Advent Calendar for the Salvation of the Planet Earth

Channelled by
'DEMARA'

(Linda Joslin)

GATEWAY BOOKS, BATH, UK.

First published in 1995
by GATEWAY BOOKS,
The Hollies, Wellow,
Bath, BA2 8QJ

(c) 1995 Linda Joslin

Distributed in the U.S.A. by
Atrium Publishers Group,
3356 Coffey Lane,
Santa Rosa, CA 95403

Cover design the Design Studio of Bristol
Cover printed by Potten, Baber & Murray of Bristol
Set in $10^1/2$ on $12^1/2$pt Bembo by Oak Press of Castleton
Text printed by Redwood Books of Trowbridge

British Library Cataloguing-in Publication Data:
A catalogue record for this book is
available from the British Library

ISBN 1-85860-033-2

Contents

Publisher's Foreword

Is it inconceivable to contemplate geophysical disaster on a scale that could sweep away coastal cities and millions of people? In fact, we forget that this has happened before, and within human memory. The Earth is the planet of free will, and humanity has already been given several opportunities to choose its own path. When these have not succeeded, Mother Earth has had to cleanse herself before the next learning experience of humanity could proceed.

The *Advent Calendar for the Salvation of the Planet Earth* is a powerful advocate for this view. The source of the book's teaching is primarily the Archangel Raphael, and other higher beings who identify themselves as Master Kathumi, Master Hilarion, Archangel Gabriel, Archangel Uriel and Archangel Michael. It was scribed, initially with some hesitation, by Linda Joslin, who channels as Demara.

Man has plundered Mother Earth. We have not honoured her sacredness; indeed, our 'civilised' cultures do not even recognise that she is our Mother or that she is alive. The destruction of the environment which causes the fish to die and the mammal kingdom to harbour sickness is not from pollution as such, but from energy imbalances. Certain parts of the land have now such bad energy that the Earth will have to purge them thoroughly. One of the main focuses will be the cleansing of the waterways and the oceans. The energy grid is not working properly. It will have to be recharged to come into harmony with the universal energy grid.

The energies are rising fast. Earth is undergoing birthing pains, and she is undertaking her own cleansing, much of which is in the form of extreme weather effects. Some are being called as light-workers to perform conscious service to aid the Earth's transition to the Fifth dimensional frequency. (This is the frequency in which many of our cousins live in other parts of the Universe.)

The world power structures still show total belief in economic growth and consumerism. Life patterns show that real lessons are only learned in adversity. Those who are unable, or choose not to submit to the new energies will not prosper in the new environment.

They will resist the changes, and will be unable to adapt to the new energies; some of them will experience the devastation wrought on those areas of negative karma that will suffer the most cleansing, and will leave the planet, still Third dimensional prisoners.

The world and people are being transformed. The scenario presented by the Masters cannot be fixed in all its detail, for the actions that we take in response to the changes are part of the solution. Don't be unduly alarmed, therefore, when Hilarion makes a prediction that has not happened, or speaks of some earth change happening in a certain year. As Hilarion says in Chapter 11, talking about time: *'We cannot give you exact amounts of time that will indicate when and where the great earth-mass changes will occur, but we can indicate the extreme areas of change; we will be adjusting the information as we go along. . . . Don't be alarmed if what we say is going to take place at that precise time. . . . Timing is a man-made entity; it holds no credence within the universal continuum'.*

We are told that transfers of energy are made in order to raise the vibrational levels so that the physical changes are possible; these changes can sometimes follow much later in time. They also tell us that the severity of possible earth changes have in some cases been reduced because of the positive activities of dedicated people.

The strong message that the *Advent Calendar* brings to us is good news, for the beings of the hierarchy say: *'We did not know when we came to you that all of the planet had fallen asleep'.* They retell Plato's myth of the prisoners in the cave who believe their shadow-world to be the only reality. Indeed, we live in a world of illusions: that humanity is alone in the Universe and at the top of the evolutionary tree; the only reality is the physical; that the individual ego and his possessions are the most important criteria; that this life is all there is, and that consciousness is extinguished upon death. We are now being called to wake up. Those whose investment is in the world of illusion may well fear transition into an unknown territory. But to gain our rightful place in the Divine scheme can only bring joy and fulfilment to humanity.

Many are aware that a crystal can hold energy – so can a book. This book carries an energy which activates the codes within us. We have been at pains not to change the meaning by the usual editing process.

They speak sometimes in metaphor. Each person is likely to gain different insights. It is very hard for us, living in the Third dimension, to begin to understand what is involved in a dimensional shift; some indications are given as to how to work with the new energies. They describe the earth changes in a way that dispels fear, and gives one a glimpse of the extraordinary heaven-on-Earth that is the destiny of this planet.

We have the privilege of being incarnate at the time of transition of the whole planet from a Third dimension environment to a Fifth, and we have the choice of helping Mother Earth cleanse herself of the energy pollution created by humanity. We inhabit the only planet of 'free choice', and we can choose now to be of service to both the Mother and the Godhead.

On a more personal note: In 1968 I had a clear vision of earth changes on the scale that are discussed in this book, and have since had further 'glimpses' of change which I have found hard to share with others. This important book demonstrates that humanity will not survive without being transformed, and that the Earth is sick and must heal herself. Our fear comes from ignorance and from self-centredness. We must learn to recognise the fruits of humanity's liberation.

It shows how we are prisoners of our limited environment. But there is no such thing as a free ride. It seems that we are in the time of the Revelation of St John – of the Apocalypse – a time to be judged. The *Advent Calendar* is addressed to humanity and offers very practical suggestions of how we, as individuals and groups, can begin to change rigid minds and our materialistic lifestyles, our relationships with one another, and open up to the Infinite.

Introduction from the Masters

For some time now you have all become used to the mastery of the planes of your physical Earth. This mastery was not what we would call mastery. The evolution of your race as a people is now in doubt. It will come about that the peoples of your planet will now undergo their true mastery initiation - that of becoming people of the Universe.

When you become people of the Universe, then you will truly understand the word 'mastery'. At the present time you are likened to those who have their heads deeply buried within the sands. You do not know of where you came from or indeed where you are going. We will be your guiding light through the years ahead of you on the Earth planet. Do not be afraid of the 'doom and gloom' scenarios that are being spoken of throughout your planet. We have come to aid you through to the truly spiritual dimensions of your minds. In doing so we must instruct you of the many changes that are about to occur. We do not give 'doom and gloom'; we will only give you the answers to the questions that have for so long been dormant within your brains and minds. In doing so we are also giving you the questions. We cannot now wait for your minds, brains and hearts to awaken; we will awaken you ourselves.

When this period of great transformation is over, then you will understand why this had to occur. You will not understand before this time. What is required now is that you begin to come along with us on this journey of great joy and happiness. This is not the sort of happiness to which you are used. We speak now of true happiness, not that which is dependent upon the goods that you accrue, or upon the dealings that you have within your great power struggles upon the earth plane. This reorganisation will allow you all of the privileges that are yours by divine right, those of greatness of spirit, universal holiness and divine integration.

As the time approaches, we beseech you to become respectful of the workings of the great universal Mind.

This manuscript has been given through one of your people in order that a full manifesto is present upon the earth planet whilst these changes are occurring.

For some this will be the first wake-up call they have received. For others it will serve as confirmation of that which they are already aware. It will be a brief recourse for us to tell you that everything that has been given will take place. As one event occurs, then it will become very much dependent upon the amounts of energy that are released as to whether the other events occur at the precise times we have mentioned.

Pretending that we do not exist is no way to call upon our mastery to assist you. We exist.

Before too long there will be many who do not wish to turn back the clocks, but who will wish that they did not have to obey the laws of the One. We cannot assist these people. Those who obey the law of the One will travel on through to the Fifth dimension on time.

For ever and a day will be a response that we would wish would appear on the lips of all of you. We wish that you become as one.

It is in our interest that you are perfectly clear as to how this material has arrived on your planes of the Earth dimension. Because of the need to receive this material as accurately as possible, we have trained our medium to receive through the areas of the brain known to you as the cerebral cortex. For some this is a process which requires the act of relinquishing all consciousness within the cerebral cortex and producing the effects of a trance state. For our medium it has been possible to receive this information whilst in a conscious state. As the information has been received, she too has been given the chance to wake up and decode the codings within her own blueprint.

As our lives become one, then you will be able to coordinate together within the multi-dimensional planes which span the Universe.

We have come in order for our knowledge to be given to all of you. As we speak, so we are with you. Advent Calendar for the Salvation of the Planet Earth – channelled through from the planes of the seventh ray by the Archangels Raphael, Michael, Gabriel and Uriel, and Masters Kuthumi and Hilarion, presided over by Lord Sananda.

BOOK ONE

The Beginnings of the Contact from Beyond

Chapter 1.

April 1990

Take heed of your thoughts, your notions, at all times; for it is through this medium that you will receive your best guidance. Be forewarned that your fate is at destiny's door. Be not thwarted by hatred, indecisions or blunders on the part of others. Be extremely careful that you take the direct route, the route that comes from your heart. I am at will to say that old habits die hard, and harder when your mind is unclear. Take up the disciplines that have stood you in good stead in the past, for you know the ways of the warrior. Be hearty in your approach, for forewarned is forearmed. Be not a victim of your own misadventures. Adventures are wondrous events in your life – pictorial escapes from the norm, from the humdrum events that cloud vision. Pictures tell a story, a wondrous one that in some ways may be thought foolhardy, but nevertheless have their apt endings and beginnings and wonderings. Please do not throw away your undertakings from so long past, for the sake of those who falter on the path. To be foolhardy would be somewhat pointless.

There is much I can accomplish through you, but you must keep the channels wide open. Remember, we come through you, not because of you, but through an awareness of you. You reach us on the higher plane of thought, but do not always respond to our instructions. We are subtler elements of the Earth plane, always there, always contactable. Keep your distance when you are not receptive, for we are forewarned of your misadventures, but cannot help you then. Be accurate in your accounts of these learning days, for they will forearm you and those who come after. Be alert at all times to your own calculations of the unknown worlds, for the calculus workings are there for you to understand, be it a hard and arduous path for those daring to follow.

I smile down on you. I am the smile of many lifetimes.

We have much information to give through your channel, but we need you to remain inactive, calm, translucent, in order for us to feed the information through fluid. Be not afraid of changes in your life, the jolts, mishaps, misadventures, for you are forewarned and fore-armed for the time ahead. We will talk in depth of the happenings to the Earth planet, of the miscalculation in energy transference, in calculating too far for too long. There is an inner buzzing that should be listened for, a vibrational warning system that is yet to be dis-covered. Be aware of the small changes to the planet's atmospheric conditions, the raindrops, the cloud formations. There will come a time when you will be able to tell the least vibrational pull that is being placed upon you and tether your outer world to the extremities of the inner kingdom.

Do not be put off by the incongruity of the language. We do not ask you to understand, just to repeat.

May 1990
Qu: How do I progress from this point?
You progress from your vantage point, from the point of wisdom from within. Your daily tasks are numerous, your nightly learnings vast. Leave time for those things that are not of this lifetime, those times of reminiscing the lifetime energies that you bring forth.

Qu: How can I best do this?
You best do this as you do other things, with love and joy and old techniques; use them wisely, for they will serve you well.

Qu: What specific techniques can I use and where do I find them?
You will find them in the repertoires of the ancient miracle makers; the cosmic giants that came before you. Hercules the lion tamer brought forth the strength from many lifetimes. He captured the strength of the lion for himself.

You will be given the answers to all your questions in due course. Be watchful of the time, for we are forewarned of doom and gloom to come. There will be long periods of disillusionment and despair, long periods of stagnation for the world at large. Periods when all seems lost. The perils at sea and on the land will be vast; many will be sucked into the mainstream of disaster. One after another you will see your major cities enveloped in flame, fire and brimstone, resulting from many Earth connections disconnecting. One after the other, cities will die. The mainstream of society will be washed upon the rocks to be discarded as forces unknown leash their power upon the Earth. Your fathers before you have known this devastation, but none alive today will understand the forces, the power. We will remind you of those times gone past, for they will aid you with the tools of knowledge needed now.

Our words are many, our facts visual; be forewarned of this impending apocalypse, for though you may wear the cap, it must fit. We have much to do to prepare your channel; our nightly workings will be vast, our daily passovers great. It is in this time that you will receive your appreciation of the intent of your Master. Be fair of heart and wise in spirit, and peace will reign over your household and your mouthpiece will be prepared.

We will come through you in order to draw up the minute details of the hierarchy that has come before you. Be not afraid of our words, there is much for you to learn. We are not of your world; we congregate on the higher planes of thought. We have much to do in order for you to learn our ways. Be not afraid; our workings come not from your earthly planes; they are far less daunting than the task that lies ahead of your fellow man.

Be aware of your every thought as you pass over the earthly plane. You are too afraid of the mishaps that will help to emerge your inner spirit . It is only through major transferences that we can make our world known to you. Much is to be learned on the higher planes of thought.

We must continue with our story, a story that will be countlessly told as time passes us by. We must be keen to put right the wrongs that have been done to the Earth; your wrongs are our own misfortunes. It is your chance as a nation to show that through decline and fall, new horizons can be brought forth. It is in our interest to maintain safety for the British at the moment. You must project ahead in order to forewarn other nations of the impending changes. You have much to do on the home front. Your warning systems are defunct. They will not pick up the higher energies needed. There is a need for breadth of vision, a complete all-encompassing perspective of the world. All energies present must be perceived.

You must complete many other tasks. The tasks that lie ahead are vast and must be dealt with one at a time. First is the accomplishment of 'duality of planes'. This will be made available to you. First, you will see us and speak to us; we come forward to you. Our messages are simple. We do not encode, we have formulas to give which must be obeyed; it is the only way. Your forefathers knew of these codes of practice. They honoured and obeyed them. 'Our Father who art in heaven, hallowed be Thy name; Thy kingdom come on Earth as it is in Heaven.'

We speak to you of much rainfall, more than has been known before. It will all come at once, out of nowhere. The spiritual powers that be will force this cleansing; the floodgates will be open.

August 1990

We wish you to write now, our words will be familiar to you. Our wishes and desires are three-fold; spiritual, mental and physical. We do not become involved with emotions. Our world is devoid of this function. Be prepared to sow the seeds with these words. They are not words that will delight the world, but will cause the imbalances necessary for action. Our words will not be hasty. They will be well thought out and concise in their approach.

We begin at the beginning, so that we may enjoy the source of our own discovery. It is a wondrous world, and there are many wondrous beings present. We must bless ourselves and our friends for their presence here today. It is too long a task for us to give the details of the minutest changes in the world's surface. It must suffice that we begin at a point where the world's balance slid from its natural choice. Many men have tethered the Earth to their own power. They have used the resources for their own ends. It has been a time for expansion, but also one of destruction. We must now redress the balance, slowly, so that the Earth may heal her own waters. I will give you now a project that will help to aid the fight against the waterways. It is one that may be considered fanciful, but will give back the energy resources that are needed in the world. You will have to explain to the scientists that it is not pollution as such, but energy imbalances that cause the fish to die and the mammal kingdom to harbour sickness.

Qu: How can we balance the energy in the waterways?
This can be carried out very simply, by immersing sulphur and carbon dioxide into the water. The sulphur will produce a cleansing effect which will also change the static condition of the water. The carbon dioxide will help to maintain the condition of all algae and other plant life in the bulk of the water. This cleansing action will cause a sediment which will fall to the bottom of the ocean and remain untouched in the main.

Qu: Can this system be used for both fresh water and sea water?
Yes, it will be easy at first to use this method in small streams and waterways, but at some length it will be discovered that large areas of the ocean bed can be caused to cleanse themselves by the immersion of nets of sulphur blocks and the insertion of self-perpetuating carbon dioxide rods. This operation will be carried out in much secret because of the threat of war missions on all banks of the tidal waterways.

Qu: How do we obtain the large sulphur blocks?
These can be obtained from the mineral kingdom. It is an element that is widely used in commercial industry.

Qu: How long before this information can be given to those who may implement it?
It will be five years before the end of the millennium that our powers of thought will be implemented.

August 1990
We must write of the great escape from the collapse of the world. This is an event that will come about because of much energy input now. It is important for all those who eagerly await the changes to

know that how they think now will change the world. It is the most important thing. We look now for control, for through control you may master your thoughts. Through thought control you master the world. Your thought patterns must be changed from the insignificant ones controlled by negative mentality to the higher degrees of spiritual acknowledgement. Your paths here will cross many times with the past, for before you the spiritual masters who conquered 'thought' have walked. I acknowledge now that the task ahead is a difficult one, but one that can be conquered.

Qu: Is there any more information on the cleansing of the waterways?
No, we have much other information to give you. We will prepare the way for toxic wastes to be laid to rest for good. At the moment there is much concern on your planet about toxic materials used by both industrial and private users. This problem can be overcome by using these materials together with neutralising substances. The substances are widely available in the same fields. As Nature chooses her materials well so that the natural action of decay takes place, so may the manufacturers do likewise. At the moment they think only in linear lines, one at a time; they manufacture, then consider the problem of destruction. This problem can be overcome now through guidance and conscious understanding of the whole problem.

We have forebodings. Your system of warning of electrical shocks is not properly aligned. The Earth contains many particles of mica which absorb and reflect electricity. It is through this way the Earth becomes overcharged. Electronic surges of power are obtained this way.

Qu: Are the scientists aware of this point?
Yes, and no. Their haphazard warning system lets them down time and time again.

Qu: Is this to do with earthquakes?
Yes, and no. It is to do with minor surges of power. These minor changes set off the major ones. Your system relates only to the surges of power which escape in the main stream. The minor streams must be monitored. One by one they must be monitored to govern the larger ones. It is possible before too long for your system to become

like a fast reactor which will record the measurement of prolonged delayed reactions, which will mean more safety for your people. It has been known for some time that the answer does not lie between the plates, but above and beyond them. There is a vast expanse of Earth which governs the power of the earthly explosions. This must be monitored. Above and beyond this the mastery of the Earth is at your fingertips. It will take much convincing of the higher powers on your plane of earthly existence before the trouble will subside.

Chapter 2.

June 1991

We have come to tell the world that our forebodings will take place as forecast. There will be much to do, and much for you all to participate in when the time comes. We are at liberty to give you much information on this matter, but must wait until we have forewarned you of the mishaps that will take place if you leave your participation too late. It has come about that many energies are now re-centring around the world. These energies cannot now be realigned. Your participation is needed to re-centre these energies.

There will be much devastation and disaster if you do not all act now. I have been given three years in which to help the Earth parties play their rightful roles. In this time there will be much guidance from the heavenly planes. After that you will be fighting the battle on your own. Our help is at hand in order to for you to assist this re-centering of the Earth energy system. It is imperative that each centre of mainstream energy is diverted into the positive cosmic ray field. We will adjust our mainstream energy to aid this diversion.

Our reports on the disturbed energy system will be spoken many times over many years, but action must take place now. Be not afraid to repeat our spoken words, for they will play a large part in bringing about the balance that is needed. Our spoken word will be adjusted from time to time, in order to bring the understanding that is needed for our instructions to be carried out. We will adjust as necessary to the minds of the people on your planet. We cannot and will not adjust the essence. Disaster is looming up on your planet and must be diverted if you are all to survive in the life form as you know it.

Be not afraid of the responsibilities that lie ahead. You will be supported from many planes, some that you know, some that you do not. Our answers to your questions on how we can divert these mainstream energies will be somewhat different to your present understanding. We will assist you to open your minds to a different jargon. Our problem now is one of adjusting to the capacity of your minds, so that we may interplay through the levels of consciousness that bind us, but do not assist us with conveying our message in a clear and precise way.

We are at liberty to say that much has been missed in the past. Your understanding does not carry the capacity to understand the subtler states of energy interplay. We are being forced to 'show our faces' more in a symbolic way. It is fair to say that much work is already being carried out by those who have some understanding of energies, but the pace must quicken. Our answers will come to you as you work, as you sleep and as you play. You must be ready to receive our spoken word at any time. We are forced by the magnetic energies to perceive the need for connection at any time.

There will be much suffering around your Earth planes in the years to come. Some will be offset by the mutual suffering. It is always easier if there are others who are affected too, but you do not as yet understand the word suffering. It is one that is used glibly amongst you earthlings. Our word for suffering is also defeat. Defeat means giving up your role in the vaster plan that is set out for you. You do not need to suffer. You need to participate in the cosmic cleansing of your globe. There is much to do and much to say. We will visit you again and again until the connection is clear; then we will stay with you. We must bridge the gap between your world and ours in order to correct the interference.

[Much information was given to me during the following year, 1992, to help re-centre energy centres, particularly in Wales, considered to be one of the 'safe' places for the future.]

June 1992
We need to speak to you of many things, things that will come to pass. It is our duty to tell you that our plans have gone wrong. The

timing is now of paramount importance. We awakened your minds, but not your hearts, to the plight of the planet. Our message comes to you from our hearts. We assumed it would touch yours. Our world is not of your world.

It came to pass a long time ago that an undertaking was 'signed' by all concerned, to bring about the passing of the old and the re-establishing of the new on your planet. The time has now come to establish the new. The energies will be realigned in many places over the next few years. The energies are already re-sited. During this time there will be much devastation and realignment of people and places. Do not be afraid of this. We have spoken to you many times of the upheavals in the world. These are also reflected in your own personal lives; much clearing away, much paying of debts owed from previous lifetimes. It is the same pattern. The Earth planet has undoubtedly paid her debts now. Have you? All over the world the stripping away will cause much chaos and havoc, but you will look at this as good, not evil. As time passes, you will understand our words.

August 1992
The culmination of 11/11 energy; this in itself is an event. The energies present now will fade, and another extremely powerful energy field will emanate around the planet's surface. This will begin in June 1996. This energy is a finer, more complex energy structure. It is one that will bring about the changes on the Earth's surface, and within the Earth's structure. We must allow you to use this energy as part of your shield. The energy will gather in small pockets at first, allowing certain areas to become more easily identifiable. Later on in that year the energies will build to extremely powerful proportions. This will be when the events are propelled into action.

We are at liberty to say that much scaremongering is taking place. The cataclysmic actions that will take place will be much as you imagine, but on a smaller scale than is in your minds at present. Our plan is to restructure the earth masses so that they form a more symbolic shape. Some say that our actions are demonic. They come from the highest quarter. We do not need to confirm to you that ours is the highest intent, but you must be aware that there are others who do not and cannot understand this. We will endeavour over the next three years to explain our workings to those of you who can understand, and to those of you that have a mind that is able to understand.

Much of the 'disaster' will be centred around areas that have gathered negative karma. This negative karma has been building a stock of energy for a very long time, and this will now be released. It will cause the clearing of old energy lines, and then in the future the 'building' of new finer energy lines. Our cataclysmic action will be one of great proportions, but nevertheless is still 'right action'. We will endeavour to give you pre-warning of any such events. Our instructions to you will be presupposed as warnings. This system will awaken in you much fear at first, but later, as events take place, you will be forewarned only to allow your minds to integrate this information. You will need no 'warning', as you will have adjusted to the sequences of events. Our main writings will be given as a synopsis of these events in detail.

We have spent many long years addressing similar material to the world at large, but to no avail. We know now that this information must arrive on time. Our discussions will continue this way for a long time. You must be prepared to receive this information contentedly. We are at liberty to say that the master plan is coming to fruition now on time, as planned. There is no escape. For those who do not believe us there will be much unnecessary stress and disbelief at the time. We are attempting to counteract some of this for some people who are needed, but we will have some that fall by the wayside.

Our many armies of light-workers are working now at this moment, so that the world will remain on her axis. Many factors are present at this moment in time that will affect the world in orbit. She has many readjustments to make. Some are large, some are small. In proportion we know that the movements you as human beings are making are as large. It would be selfish of us not to understand that the transition for you as a people will be an enormous task, but our salvation is that some of you will make it, and be a part of the new beginning. We must hasten to add that our species will be able to follow through with you. Our domain is being altered too. We have now much freedom of thought and practice, but because of the Earth's dilemma, we have been commanded from the highest powers to assist throughout the coming years. Our freedom is your freedom. In time to come you will understand much more of the workings of other dimensions.

We are at liberty to say that the oncoming months will be activated by the impulse of your group workings. We can see now that the growth needed is one of complete surrender, surrender to the oncoming plan of events and most of all surrender within yourselves. Our objective is to allow your individual spirits to become more alive, more resourceful and also more dynamic. Becoming light-workers has in the main been part of all of your lives, but not so much light-workers for the world, but on an individual ego basis. You are now all being asked to continue to be light-workers, but in the true sense of the word. Workers of light for the sole purpose of light. Beacons from the inner world shining through you in order to diffuse light energy into every corner of the Earth's circuitry.

Delay in attaining this state of being will mean more darkness, and therefore more death and destruction. Delay will also entail much stress for you all on a day to day basis. Surrender will come about some time after you realise the need for it. It is not a state which comes easily to the humanoid brain cells or mind.

Diffused energy is seen emanating all around the planet; small sparks of energy that could be contained and channelled into direct action. A source of much confusion is seen, as direct action is delayed by mind and ego interference. Any interferences will delay our interplay with you.

Many particles of matter are held together by adverse forces. This means that as we unleash the hold of adverse forces, then we will see the breaking up of various solid forms both in the Earth's structure and in the physical assemblance around the planet. Much of what you have built has been formed in a negative way. The centres of old energy were not built around sacred sites, but around sacred ritualistic areas. The time for ritual is over, the time for purity of spiritual intent and therefore guidance is here. We have the information you need in all areas of your 'work'. We therefore dedicate ourselves to our task to assist in this stage of humanity's evolvement through to the real spiritual realms.

We can only assist you when you are open to learn. Your control of your own minds is part of the major problem that we have to contend with. Because of the objectives that you have set yourselves within your life patterns, you are still held so very much onto the lower consciousness levels. In order to release these you must plan a pattern that is now one of the utmost highest intent, both for yourselves and the planet. These new patterns can be implanted into your minds so that the highest consciousness levels can be obtained.

It is not an easy path, but none of you has a choice. This choice is one that none of you also want to let go of. Man's lifespan has been one very much of individual choices and chance factors. Chance factors have also played somewhat a larger part than should have been. On the higher levels chance does not play a part. Your life patterns become one of devotion to the highest realms and devotion to your spiritual natures.

February 1993
We are agasp ourselves at the incredible energy that is upon your planet now. This energy is not just from the outer planes, but is exploding from within the very source of the Earth's crust. This energy build up is not readjustable, it is only comparable to what we had imagined. The energy explosion will be much greater than had originally been anticipated. Our attempts to readjust earlier have become thwarted. We can now only instruct you as human beings to align with your God forces. This is the only salvation.

We find it interesting that only a small minority of the star-seeded ones are yet ACTIVATED. They must wake up. We will activate them one way or the other. The 'other' does not carry much justice – it is forced action. This will come about within the ensuing three years. Our major plan of action is to be at peace with you, not at war.

Our amazement as to the whereabouts of some of the star-seeded ones must be spoken of. We need to readjust their lives now, but can not do so until they make themselves known to us. We only have CONTACT with 80% of them at present. We hasten to add that many 'peoples' are thinking they are star-seeded and they most definitely are not. The star-seeded ones are encoded with the dynamics of our plan; they do not need to think about it, they are only readjusting the dials of their inner computers to relay the information from within their own encoded system. Much has been forgotten, much has been lost, but only within the physical dimensions; once encoded, never forgotten.

Much time has been taken up with this master plan for the Earth planet. We have reassembled much of the White Brotherhood, the Ashtar command and the elders of the planet Earth to assist her now. Gaia has had many lifetimes caught in the web of destruction, assisting other planets in their growth, altering to the misaligned cosmic soup around her. She now rests in her own cosmic consciousness.

This period of activity of earthlings upon the planet surface has been her reproductive period. She has been in gestation for the 'nine months'. We would estimate that the birth is coming. Our projections for her are that the ensuing birth will harmoniously cleanse her waterways; her awkwardness of motion will be corrected, her balance will return. The motion with which she dances around the Universe will now become an activation of the Christ spirit. He dances not with an awkward gait, but spirals and glides as if commanded by the light energies of life itself. It will be a wondrous sight. The ghostly overtones of times gone past will disappear as if they never existed.

Much assistance is needed, as in every birth on your Earth plane, we need to clear the way now for the birth canal to be opened. The channel for this will consist of many hosts of beings, hosts of beings who will breathe with her as she manipulates her energies to the task ahead. Labour pains are not easy to cope with. Her labours will be long and unfulfilling at first. It is as if she is in the death throes; her awkward gait does not help the birth.

We will construct a girdle of energy around her so that not too much energy escapes. Any escaping gases will only help to clear the birth canal. Her control at this time will be adjusted by the energies that are fed in by the people on the planet breathing with her. You know how to breathe – you must allow yourself to adjust your breathing with her. She needs comfort and support of the highest and most gentle kind. Our support is unanimous, yours must be the same.

The 'angels' that are present around the planet now are praying for her successful completion. You must pray also. In prayer you will join with the God forces and command the correcting of wrong action. Align now to the highest powers that you can attract around you. It is the misfortune of some that their energies are not aligned enough even to attract their own destiny.

Chapter 3.

It is unusual for the star-seeded to be now attracted to the path of karma, but unfortunately some are sadly falling by the wayside. Their grief will be when they realise that too much time has lapsed for them to carry out their activation. As for the 'fate' of those who did not determine during this lifetime to address these important issues, then they will wander on through many more lifetimes of dusk and light, of mutation of their soul blueprint.

A profound change will occur for some. These are the people who, although they did not choose to be star-seeded, will nevertheless return to their Fifth dimensional selves. They will be greatly assisted by the oversouls who will be present on the planet over the next four years. It is estimated that the rebirthing process will be extremely painful when one does not consciously assist. Many souls will be thrown against the rocks; thrown against the rise and fall of the incredible ocean energies as they break forth, swamping the Earth's surface with many more gallons of water than you have ever experienced before. More souls will be hung up to the vultures because of the chaos and confusion.

You will see a madness take hold, as Mother Earth cries out in pain. Her pain is also your pain. The star-seeded ones can anaesthetise her labour. You can make it easier for her. As you breathe you will be able to attract the energy needed to convulse her energies to play out their destiny. You will be assisting the destruction of the Third dimensional life on this planet; will you play your parts?

It has been a long journey on the Earth plane for all of you. You have sacrificed your spiritual mantle in order to learn from these deathly planes. We must now be of service to the world, but from our spiritual standpoint. We cannot help humanity in any other way. It is sacrifice now of the earthly planes for all of you. Some will go to the barriers of the extremities of the earth plane challenge before they will let go and return to their spiritual mantle. We must challenge this now, before it is too late for them to return. Our procedures for bringing back those people who have already gone too far into decadence is not pleasant. We must now retrieve all, one way or another.

Forgive us for the challenging material that will be given to you. We cannot save you from the knowledge that will be bestowed upon you. You must sacrifice your peace of mind on the earthly plane in order to comply with our orders. Be not afraid of our words. We cannot be on guard for your sake; it is for the sake of humanity that we speak. Crucifixion has taken place before on your planet Earth. It will take place again, but not for the same reasons. We are at liberty to say here that man does not take his own life. It is not within his own power to do so. He is always aided and abetted by those from other planes, to do so.

Be not afraid of this cataclysmic action. You are forewarned of the affray that will beset your planet. In time to come you will understand the gravity of our words. We too are aggrieved at the limits to which humanity has stooped, but we must now be aware of the saving grace that will be activated at this time. The warriors of the Christ spirit will be activated by the higher planes. You must go into action to clear the Universe of the decadence that befits those who disastrously claim their rights to power and malicious effects. Many of you who carry the Christ mantle will realign very shortly through the ascension process.

The time has come for the four corners of the Earth to realign with the polarity of the spiritual hemisphere. Our time has come to assist in this realignment. Your time has come to be present, both in physical form and spiritual alignment with us.

It is true that both the stratosphere and the atmosphere of your planet are becoming too sick to serve the human race. We can do nothing about this as our powers are too strongly connected to the Godhead to be of use on the physical plane. We cannot adjust the physical plane without first readjusting the spiritual plane. Our forces are ready to be used to redevelop the planet on the Fifth dimensional level. We can but try to educate those who are willing participants in this process of evolution.

Nothing will stop us now. We must complete our task. Before too long it will be too late to readjust those who need readjusting. We speak of those who have made no movement in their lives to realign with their spirituality. Because of this situation, we must ask that you disconnect from any of the people that are going in the direction of darkness. It is not easy to seek out those who are blinded by their own power, from those who are just mildly intoxicated by it.

You must readjust your own lives in order to be present when the time comes to play your parts in this major event in the Earth's history. Being present does not mean just in the physical form. You must be present in the moment so that you catch the 'bus' when it comes.

March 1993

You must adjust your lives now to include much of the creative arts. The time has come for allowing life to give you what you really want. Much work has been carried out in the field of healing, but now the time approaches when others will need to hear the spoken word. Our adaptation of the events that will be heralded upon the planet Earth will be heard from here to the other side of the world. We must acclaim our part in the salvation of the planet. She will be assisted by many who do not know the true extent of this master plan, but we will attempt to make clear all the information that is needed, so that the main attraction is going to be one of 'duality versus credibility'.

Beyond this point of interaction lies a master plan for the cosmos. It is beyond your comprehension at this point in time. It is adrift from any concept that you have addressed in previous lifetimes. The master blueprint is being activated from many levels. We will attempt to steer you in the correct direction as things begin to manifest on the Earth level of activity.

Many souls will be reactivated at the moment when the molten lava begins to flow. We cannot adjust now those who seemingly accept the disastrous scenarios being enacted on the planet. We must adjust as people become aware of the need for readjustment. The molten lava flow will no doubt bring fear to the surface, and for some this will be enough to reactivate their blueprints. This fear will not be on a level that has been felt before, for none of you have really experienced fear in the real sense.

Our 'glue pot' is being activated. This means that we have the power to enable the star-seeded ones to be literally glued to the mainstream energies. This means that although they will be present during the ensuing battle, they will be very much exempt from the throes of the negative energy forces. There will be present, always, during the next four years, much positive flow of energy, but in order to align to this field you must have raised your spirits in the direction of the archangels. We can then guide you to the areas that will not be devastated. We can also protect you.

The 'fall-out' of energy debris will be great. There will be great manifestations of power misuse. This will be led in the main by a body of people who fear 'God and the wrath of God'. They will be stopped, but not until the energy subsides. As man reunites with the Godhead, then others will come to clear away the torment of the years gone by. We will be carrying out a salvage operation, but must ask that no members of the public assume this as their objective. The objective of those that survive the effects of the unleashing of the negative energy forces will be one of utmost intent on the spiritual plan ahead.

We have no objection to you now forming collectives that carry on the work of purifying the planet; but only now can this be a plan of purification through ejection, not through condensing down or solidifying. We must help you to understand that our plan of action is now one of redemption only through the cataclysmic actions that are now upon you. Be prepared to stand away from the groups that still attempt to purify and solidify the planet's resources. She has become very much intoxicated with negativity, and must now be given the opportunity to eject these energies.

As time goes on, it will become apparent to you that all the energies from the last two thousand years have become very decadent and mouldy. They must be cleansed from the Earth's surface and from within the Earth's interior. We are about to assist this 'spring cleaning' operation. It will be spring when the energies release the extremities of the negative energy forces. It will be spring when the energies that are hidden within the Earth's interior become mobilised and begin to seep out, rising to a large crescendo as 'she', the planet Earth, gasps for new breath, new life and new energy. Transformation will be achieved.

Honesty is a form of transformation. It is only through the upholding of our honesty that we can perform the miracles that need to take place, at this time, on the planet's surface. Honesty is a form of self-expression. It is very powerful to perform the exercises that are given in one of the excerpts of the New Bible edition, of Genesis. These exercises excite the patterns encoded into the human DNA structure that must awaken. The exercises themselves are patterned to become useful as a tool of SELF-expression. Many people have become immersed in self-improvement techniques which allow only the mind to realign, not the spirit.

The codings which are present in every human being are on a spiritual level, not on a human mind level. This activation will be immersed in trials and tribulations as people try their hardest to understand. But the understanding will only come about when the spirit has become involved, and then only when the process is complete. Understanding is only fruitful when we begin to see that our Universe is full of irregular patternings that, once freed, will enable the new, finer energies to bounce forth. Patternings have existed for thousands of generations in order for the Universe to be bound in form. Our master plan is to release all of these patterns. Therefore, all the full creative power of the Universe will flow free. We do not expect you to understand the complexity of this state, because it would endanger your mental capacities. Just know that we will be assisting you until you reach the Fifth dimensional state of being.

It is now very appropriate for you to understand the workings of the planetary energy system. Against the laws of the universal system, many planets have broken through the ancient barriers, erected in order to stop negative energy flow. These barriers were built up over eons of time in order to protect the Earth planet and other planets within her category. Because of the energy release from the other planets, we now must readjust the blueprint around planet Earth. This blueprint is similar to the humanoid blueprint, in that it holds the emergence of Fifth dimensional existence. The other planetary energies have caused much of the Earth's blueprint to become screened, screened from activation. This screening must be removed.

The ancient rituals used by warrior man in the past were very much part of the sun god ritual Ra, calling into effect the power and life force of the Sun's emanations. It is now time to call upon Ra again in order to balance the energies around the planet Earth. Because of the imbalance around the planet, we require you to administer great powers of intent to realise these energies. This energy field must be balanced before the Earth allows herself to approach the time of rebirth. Without this balancing it is possible for the waves of energy surrounding the Earth planet to spin her off into the orbit of distant moons and suns. The miraculous balance of position of Mother Earth can not be sustained when she is in the throes of rebirth. We must assist – we command you, to assist also. Our command is not one of useless demeanour, but one of the highest order.

It is incomprehensible to most of you on the planet at this moment, the complexity of what approaches . The action about to be reaped on your planet is one of the utmost power. Within this power is held the opportunity to regain your sense of 'self'. To regain your blueprint with life everlasting; everlasting in a sense of no rules, no surrounding barriers, no time limits, no hostility, no blame, guilt or fear. To bathe in a 'lifetime' of love, forgiveness, humility, honesty, salvation. It is your heritage; we bestow upon you now the right to reclaim your heritage. Pardon me for not allowing you to pass over this possibility! As mutations of the essence, you have tarried too long on these earthly planes.

The pain and suffering is now at an end. It is incomprehensible to many who are suffering that they are causing the suffering! We do not talk too loudly of this, as many are not ready to hear the words of truth and honesty. We can not afford to lose these souls because of words spoken in haste or arrogance. Our objective is to reclaim every soul on this planet that is at all able to rejoice in spirit. The mouldings will drop away as the planet throws away her Earthly mantle. She will escape from the trappings of this Earthly culture. Many souls will escape also.

The time approaches when the spoken word will be accepted from our heavenly planes. Our span of time of assistance to you will be foreshortened when we have the compliance of all star-seeded souls. We come in peace. We reign from our heavenly platform in order to bring peace on Earth. Do not be mistaken by the incongruity of our words; we do mean peace. As you continue to go about your Earthly lives, be aware of the subtle changes that are happening. It is not so difficult now to see the beauty that is hidden.

April 1993
Against our wishes there are many who gather now in groups in congruous with life itself. It is a useless exercise to now gather together in this way. At last we have some of the codings becoming decoded – now is the time to accept your independence. It is only through individual energy forces that we will become one. The groups that gather together on the lower levels of interaction are becoming less conscious. They are producing the effect of group consciousness which in itself is demonic. It does not serve the planet Earth; it can only serve itself. We are in need of individual people acting as individuals. Each individual plays a part in the great cosmic happening.

We have several important links in the chain missing. If you are one of these links then decide to play your part. We can not do without you. We have a loosely linked chain with links missing. This is not powerful. This is weak; we must complete the chain. The linkage depends on your intent, your willingness, your love. Many people are dancing around on the perimeters of this plan. They see, they hear, but they do not commit. We must have your commitment. The plan of action for the Earth remains sealed, sealed from the eyes of the non-believers. You may be a believer, but you must now become a participator. Participate in whatever way your body, mind and soul are able. We do not dictate orders. The orders are encoded into your very cells; you must reunite with these orders. Be still and hear the words being spoken. This voice speaks to you and only you. We cannot tell you of these secrets. The secret is for you to realise.

Many are now listening to their higher selves, they are journeying on through the mire, reaching their destinations ahead of time. Some are rejoicing in the knowledge, but are not moving on. They must confront their fears, align with their spirits and become the warriors of the planet Earth. In times gone past the zealots challenged the law, challenged the reign of the king. They became the outlaws of the law. The law was the law of the land, not the law of the heavens. You are now at liberty to throw away the conventional preconceived patterns through which you have lived your lives. You must now obey only the command encoded into your very souls.

You are who you are, you must begin to realise who you are. We can begin to see that some are now using other names, names that are predestined to be used, these names are encoded in you. Do not presumptuously assume that you are to be given an initiation where your 'name' will be announced. Within your own circuitry the key is held, the key to who you are. Ask yourselves now 'who am I?' The faint whisper that you hear is who you are. These names are important catalysts for you to hold yourselves on course, as you complete your passage through the final years of the Third dimensional earth field. Do you now find yourselves in confusion?

You must align now with this deeper sense of self. Ask again – who am I? When the leaves go brown and wither, something is left, some essence within the tree. This essence knows to bud forth again the following year. You must realise that your true essence has always been present in your soul. Things have not changed. You have been asleep, dreaming. Was it a nightmare? This was your time of hibernation, hibernation that brought a true cognition in the most holy sense of who you were. You have now consciously dreamed your dream awake, your time of hibernation is over. The buds must burst forth. Dance and be merry as you **choose** to live through another 'day'.

Be at one with your Universe. The time approaches when the two suns will become your gods. This will come about when the Sun has begun her cycle of rebirth. She will assist your transition. You must become aware of the power of the energy that is rained down on you from the solar system. This solar system is your power house. She has the power to destroy or rekindle the flame of life. Many now have become rigid in their way of thinking that no energy source has the power to destroy your planet. We must tell you that the Earth's crust could become aflame if the Earth's balance was adjusted to envelop her into a chosen orbit of the Sun. Many have predicted that the Sun's rays will ultimately burn their way through the Earth's crust, but none have predicted that the Sun herself will be split in two as the changes take place in the heavens above. Our estimation of the explosion can not be measured in your Earthly minds. We cannot begin to explain to you that the area affected will be grossly under-estimated by the humanoid response to existence.

The heavens are much vaster than your minds could at this time cope with. We have no notion to expand your consciousness to this degree, but in time, when you have realigned within your soul bodies we will become one mind, one life. A life force that sees all, knows all and comprehends all. Many masters have now become embedded within the energy field around your planet Earth. This energy field will enable you to become more finely attuned, so that you may join with us, exciting the attunement of the many who begin to dream their dream awake.

May 1993

The time has come for the impossible to be made possible. What we mean here is that the 'impossible' solutions in your own minds must be made manifest. It is not 'impossible' to allow the higher mind to now take control of your lives. Those of you who work also on the 'light' planes of involvement can now allow this emphasis on your lives to hold a greater portion. It is important for the whole of humanity. We do not wish you to become afraid here of respons-ibility, for we know that this is a limitation that your minds can produce. We wish that you now take responsibility, equally that you all now take your rightful places in the linkage of the chain of light. Because of the time ahead we cannot wait for this linkage to be completed.

It will be far more devastating for your planet Earth if we do not have a complete chain of light-workers. Most of you are aware now of the imminence of the plan of action, but not all of you are in your rightful places. We must endeavour to place you there ourselves. Because of the strong attraction that you all have to the light, it is not hard for us to nudge you towards the full strength beam. We just have to pull away some of your attachments to the earthly plane. This way we will be responsible for you joining our forces. At present there are thought forms present in your earthly world that endeavour to frighten you away from the light. These thoughtforms have been present for many millennia. They are present for this one. We cannot allow these thoughtforms to continue to abrade the percentage of light-workers that are presently being affected. We must now endeavour to clear away any remaining negative energy waves present in this form.

There is still much contested information about the star-seeded ones. There is a battle amongst spirit energies that find it incomprehensible to accept that there is indeed an 'elitist sect'. We have adjusted much of the information given at present to your plane of intelligence so that the way would not be too precarious for those who are indeed part of the elect or elite. Much of the information being presented at this moment has, in as much as the wording concerned, been subdued so that the delay in activation for those souls is not stretched out too far in time. Any delay now in activation would indeed cause mighty energy explosions. These energy explosions will indeed come about, but will be subdued by the light-energy workers linking the chain together.

The time has come for that chain of links to be placed around the planet's surface, so that the Earth's energies are anchored under a chain of light. This will move the Earth's energies, but only in a more positive way. It will move the energies away from the truly earthy response to a more centred response. You may find it hard to understand that the explosions of energy that the Earth will release can be positive, but positive they are. It is more commonplace for Earthlings to consider any explosion to be demonic. The best way to start addressing this escapade is to readjust now to the streams of light that are approaching the planet Earth. These streams of light need to be pulled down to the Earth's surface.

Chapter 4.

May 1993

We must now forecast ahead to the times when much change and fortitude will be needed on the planet Earth. Be aware that the information will be somewhat catastrophic, therefore you will need to be very precise when giving this information to those around you. Be aware also that we will be notifying many sources of similar details. At first the energy that surrounds the planet Earth will become very dense. This denseness is not negative; it is only the intensity of the energy that produces the density. This energy will protect the planet Earth and will enable many light-workers to proceed with the anchoring processes. This anchoring will prevent the Earth from becoming too unstable during the transitional stages of her growth. She will be torn apart physically from the interior to the exterior, but the energy field around her will enable the 'completion' process to take place. Her auric field will be adjusted over the next six months, so that the energies do not affect the balance of her motion in space.

Because of the adjustments it will be a time of great change. The rainfall will be extreme. In order to avoid the calamities of flooding one should be prepared. Postponement of preparation will cause many deaths and much destruction. We cannot adjust now the inevitable cause and effect of the great plan. Many people will adjust, but we must save as many as possible so that the proportion of peoples on the planet does not suffer unduly. Around about the end of the year there will be much rainfall again. This rainfall will begin to counteract the energy disturbances.

These energy disturbances will come about because of the aftermath of much activity on the inner planes. Rainfall helps to re-distribute energy forces that have become solidified and clogged into highly charged intense units. Because of the rainfall these intense units disperse and break down into diluted forms of energy chains. We can readjust the energy in this way, but as usual our counteraction will cause another action – much water fall. Because of the intensity of the interaction of energy and water you will also experience great lightning flashes. These lightning flashes will disturb many energy fields of the people on the planet Earth. At the time of the great storms you would be advised to readjust and centre yourselves.

Centering will help to overcome the energy dispersion that will occur as these units break down. It will be as if you were experiencing many different electrical impulses erratically pulsating at the same time. The centering exercises will tether you to the inner quarters of your own energy field, thus enabling the outer energy field to restrict the impact of the pulsating around you.

Imagine that you must protect yourselves from great heat impact; you would not reach out towards the source of the heat, therefore you must retire inside your own protection field – inside yourself. These exercises are quite simple, but should be practised now to enable you to automatically slip into this mode when being attacked from outer energy sources. These exercises will be very important now that the quickening is occurring. We must endeavour to protect your energy fields from any collision with negative rays. This exercise can be performed whenever you feel in the least affected by obnoxious fallout or energy clearance.

Be at ease in yourself by becoming at one or in attunement with your own organs. What we mean is to own these organs in conscious recognition – the heart, kidneys and liver. These organs control the system of your body. You cannot be alive without these three organs. Therefore it is important to consciously rejoice in their activity. Becoming at one with these organs will enable your system to counteract the obnoxious influences of the energy rays. You must visualise each organ in turn so that you feel the unique vibration of each organ. Then, when you have a clear picture, visualise the organ working in perfect order despite any infiltration into your own energy circuitry.

You will be programming each organ to function perfectly despite any discordant factions surrounding you. You will be producing a far superior working of the organ concerned. This will assist your transcendence into the Fifth dimensional state. Each day use this exercise to strengthen your physical body to withstand the energy forces that will penetrate your planet Earth. A few minutes each day will allow your body to crack open the limited boundaries of your physical structure.

You must be prepared to carry out all of these exercises daily; they will become as you say 'your bread and butter' of survival. You will be of no use to yourselves or humanity if you cannot cope with the effects of the energy forces. Stay away from any obnoxious energies that you do not have to be involved with. These include television circuitry. The energies currently being used are now too toxic to ensure your safety. As each little droplet of energy seeps into your energy field it is lessening your ability to build a protective field. This protective field must be secure and in place before 1994.

At the beginning of this year you will realise why we are being so explicit about the negative energy rays. The energies around computer equipment are now quite damaging to the human aura. These rays of energy penetrate and adulterate the objective of aligning with spirit. They operate on a purely logical structure and are not conducive to spirit. Any conflicting influences will weaken your resolve to activate purely on a spiritual level. We must say that although the energies are conflicting, they are also aligned to the energy pulsating into your planet and can be used to pick up signals of impending changes. It is of great use now to begin to meditate at least three times in one day; this should be morning, noon and eventide. This will give you a balance of energy flow. At the present time the energies that you use are very staccato. They stop and start, and labour under great encumbrances. If you meditate you will be monitoring the balance of energies. The energies will be allowed to flow more gently and constantly throughout your body, enabling you to remain calm and objective what ever is being experienced.

June 1993.

Many more star-seeds are needed now. We cannot emphasise too much that the missing ones will in fact affect the cataclysmic action planned. We are at present attempting to align the energy fields around the planet Earth, but our task is an enormous one. We do not believe it is possible to address many of the problems that surround the Earth planet without much unrest within the Earth's interior. Because of this much unrest is taking place within the minds of man. Our warranty here is to adjust and realign without too much affray for mankind, but this is not seemingly possible. Because of the complexity of the minds of men, we are seeing that much energy escapes towards the astral planes. Our exercise now is to realign, despite the unrest to mankind, we cannot be kind and ineffective.

We must complete the plan of rebalancing. Much water has befallen your planet over the last several days. This is a retribution in order to monitor the activity of the astral and mental sides of mankind. By activating the extreme conditions we can monitor the results of our actions. In Wales in particular there has been much sorting out of the light-workers and the 'waders'. In short we do not know how long we can hold the balance of the planet Earth in her orbit. The extreme results of this will bring about changes far ahead of time. This century will then not see the 'turn'. Hostility amongst mankind is producing varied effects upon the astral planes. Humanity will only survive if we can bring about the lightening effects in time. It will suffice to say that much of the atmosphere is polluted, much of the oceanic world is polluted. The Earth planet herself is severely challenged to survive the extreme effects of pollution.

Because of the mentality of mankind at this point in time, we must rescue more of the star-seeded ones from the mainstream of society. Our rescue work involves the cooperation of other star seeds who are already activated – be it not wholly. To be in advance of your time is the best place to be. We do not jest. We are very much activated today by the severity of the Earth's needs. The balance is teetering; she must be cloaked in light. For this we require the assistance of as many light-workers as possible. It is humanly possible to ensure that the balance does not shift before everything else is in place in the cosmic universe.

August 1993.
We move in haste. It is because of the backlash of hardened energy
that we now have to move forward in disjointed action. Be not
alarmed at the words that are used; it is because of the backward
nature of the humanoid man that our plans are backfiring, like jet
plane exhaust systems. After much listening and debating many
factions of your light-worker system are deciding that they know
more than we do. They are not prepared to align themselves solely to
the Master Rays. We cannot force them; they must readjust nearer the
end of the century. Our only concern at the moment is that we utilise
all of the main anchoring systems available to us. The fact that many
will not align soon enough to the Master Rays is not our concern.
Our system of energy will allow us to utilise all of the light-workers
to assist the anchoring of the Earth planet, regardless of whether they
will choose to ascend with her.

Many earth movements will be created over the next six months.
These will be in the form of tumultuous overflows of energy from the
Earth's interior. Southern Spain will be lapped over by many tidal
waves caused by the interior of the Earth's crust activating with the
fumes caused by the over zealous activity of radium beneath the
Earth's surface. There has been much activity beneath the Earth's
surface for many months. Now it is because of the exterior rays of
purifying energy that the inner will be forced to cleanse herself. We
cannot predict accurately times and places, but we are very much
aware of the areas most affected.

Another area that is becoming very much a 'danger spot' is in the
highlands of Scotland. This is because of the radium activity beneath
the surface in this particular area too. The radium that has been
dumped below the surface carries on a certain chemical/alchemic
reaction with the elements that are around it. It does not need to be in
the atmosphere to penetrate through the energy force field, it only
needs to be present. Very much as your Tachyon attracts and repels,
so does the radium, but in an opposite extreme way. The force field
will adjust to Tachyon beads, it will also adjust to radium energies.

Either way the universal energy force field is being manipulated beyond its capacity to emanate etheric energy patterns. The patterns must be in balance with life in order to contain the molecules and atoms to assist the growth of life and not the destruction of it.

October 1993
There are several synopses of the concurring events that are happening on the planet in several different quarters. These events are not so much cataclysmic happenings as they are smaller, but more powerful snatches of energy transferences. We must differentiate between the energy transferences and the more apocalyptic energy exchanges, because much has been said of the great changes that will come about on your planet Earth over the next coming years. The energy transferences are very much to do with the overall energy input that is being placed within the Earth's atmosphere. These energy transferences are mildly accumulating between the stratosphere and the atmosphere, in order to bring about the more catalytic changes within the overall plan.

We intend to allow you to have much more pre-warning of any alarming catalytic changes which will involve disaster areas. This is because we do not wish our mainline light-workers to be involved in these areas. We cannot command a response from any of you; we can only give you fair warning and then allow all of you to command your own response. Be not afraid of the information that will be given to you. We do not expect you to understand completely the way that this main plan will unfold. We cannot expect you, who have spent many lifetimes within the old energy system of the Earth, to suddenly comprehend the workings of the totality of the universal energy system.

Our task is to enable you all to have the opportunity to now remove the veils from your understanding and therefore proceed along the path of man without veils, which to you will seem a stormy passage. We ask only that our pathway is made as open as possible, so that we can give as much assistance as is possible at this time. Most of our time is taken up with investigating the possibilities of direct contact with more humans. We cannot adjust our plan, but can certainly adjust the outcome of human procedures that are at present leading the whole of the human race into oblivion. It is irreversible now. We do not mean that the human race will be obliterated; we are attempting to show you that the plan for the Earth is irreversible. She must now be allowed to heal herself. We do not adjust the actions of the Creator, we only adjust the actions of the predator.

Before too long there will be many side issues for you to deal with. These are likened to the spots on a face. Many issues will be coming to a head and then bursting all over the front of the pages of your newspapers. Many issues that before have not been exposed will come to the surface to be addressed by the man in the street. We do not expect you to react to these many issues, but bide your time before then addressing these issues from a higher perspective. Before too long the governments will fail because of the now disillusioned attitude of the mass of society. Upon the collapse of the governments you will be allowed to secretly open the pathways to higher consciousness for many more peoples. At present the governmental systems destroy the opportunity for many of your public to allow their minds to be opened.

We do not condemn the attitude of the public, but must chastise those who have for many generations played blind-man's bluff with those of lesser intelligence. The blindfold must now be removed. We will remove the blindfold, after that there will be much need of rehabilitation and readdressing old problems, old situations in a new format. Can you imagine what it would be like if suddenly all of the coverings were removed at once? The world would not survive in any form because of the mental harassment to the minds of men. Before too long, we will be approaching many more of your governmental figures. We cannot now wait for the oncoming slaughter of base instincts to pave the way for us.

Many of your governmental celebrities are themselves going through the energy transference changes. They do not understand themselves why they are beginning to feel differently about so many issues, and will need assistance in understanding the growing levels of consciousness being placed upon them. Our pathway to these individuals is becoming clearer and clearer because of the interference from our most beloved counterparts the extra-terrestrial beings. Many parties have been called upon to play their parts in this most magnificent plan for creation. After much confusion you will see the remnants of your governmental forces changing towards enlightenment. There will be many who will not see the necessity for change, and these people will develop there own separate power structures, becoming more and more decadent as time goes on. When one man governs his own forces in darkness then the extent to which he can go multiplies tenfold.

We do not wish to place fear in your hearts only to forewarn you of many of the side issues of this great plan that you will be dealing with. After the governmental collapses many of the old systems will be destroyed. One after another you will see your cities embroiled in disaster. Now is the time for all of you to reassess safe positioning for yourselves and your families. Do not be afraid to make diverse moves in very strange directions just because the impulse guides you there; 'you' will be right for you. At this point do not ask advice; there will be many who would have you stay in illusion – the more in illusion, the more comfortable it will be for those who do not choose to come out of it.

Throw caution to the wind. Caution has not been the best ally in your lives up to this point. We have come upon a time when caution can only govern those who will attract the disaster areas to them. If we allow ourselves to look closer at the word 'caution' – are we not talking of fear? Be at ease now with those areas of your mind that have been trying to guide you for many years. It is time now to throw caution to the wind. Be at ease also with the idiosyncrasies that you will be led to allow from your being; you are all idiosyncratic beings. You have allowed these parts of yourselves to become atrophied, and much worse in some cases, to become completely obliterated. Stand up and be counted now, for who you are, what you are and what you are about to become. We wish you much love and assure you that the grace of the lord goes with you, be at ease with this knowledge. Blessed be those who will share in these coming times of changes, both on a planetary level and a transitory energy level.

Chapter 5.

January 1994

Apart from the severe weather conditions prevailing over the planet, there are many more energy transferences that will affect certain direct areas. The effect this will have is that many more tidal waves, earth traumas and hurricanes will take place over the ensuing months ahead. Because of this there will be much need to address the public at large, not on a small scale, but within large public places and with the use of the media when ever possible. Much of what has happened will be considered minor compared to the coming apocalypse situation. It is not because of the areas themselves, but because of the energy build-up in these areas that they will be cleansed.

After the next few months you will see great changes in the minds of man. It is only through trauma that many people will change. We cannot also be responsible for this situation; our only choice is that of optimum results as fast as possible. The apocalypse situation has come about because of the fast reactor resistance. Resistance itself is expected, but what has actually happened is that many people have bedded themselves down in a new reality; the reality of 'it will be all right'. It can never be all right whilst man is incapable of seeing the overall picture. The cosmic overview must be taken into account. If it is not, things will never sort themselves out.

We are prepared to adjust where necessary on your planet until you become the people that you are destined to become. We cannot adjust your minds, only your situations. This will become more and more catalytic until the rigidity becomes flexible. We need to be able to mould your consciousness into the wholeness of the universal mind. The universal mind will become more powerful as one and all become at one. Our minds do not have that choice we are moulded with the universal mind. We are gathering in the minds of men so that there is no conflict within the galaxies. Your galaxy has much conflict within the minds of men. To be or not to be was always the question, to have and to hold have become much more the issue on your planet. We must adjust this sentiment. You are incapable of taking charge of your own planet in the state of mind that exists between governments, societies and the extra-terrestrial beings.

At some stage we will discuss with you the possibilities that exist between yourselves and these extra-terrestrial beings. There are many that visit your solar system and your planet on a regular basis, but do not make themselves known directly to you. They come to heighten the awareness around you. Their own energy can draw off negativity and re-enliven dead energy spots on the planet. These dead energy areas have to become reactivated so that the mainstream energy lines will flow smoothly. Much of this work has already been accomplished in the western world, but there are still many areas within the eastern block that are negative. These will be reactivated later this year.

During the next three months there will be much clarity amongst the hierarchy of officials carrying out the mundane task of supervising the operation of government. After this has happened the task will be to clarify their own positioning within the governmental body. You will then see many governmental officials either resign their positions or acquire another route into the source of power. It has been underestimated how far some of these figures will go to make sure that their positions of power remain stable. It is not possible now to acquire positions of power, but this will not stop some of these officials trying. Their efforts will be in vain, they will try to use methods of sheer hypocrisy to remain in power, but after the June by-elections there will be total anarchy within the parliamentary judiciary system. The only escape will be to call a general election, but we must advise you now that this will be without avail.

After the 10th of June there will be anarchy on a scale that has never been witnessed. This will be thought of as a complete breakdown of the parliamentary system as you know it today. There will be gasps of 'how did we get to this point?'. During this escapade some members will attempt to carry out great acts of great humility. It is estimated that one in every ten parliamentary candidates will receive their notice to end their term of service. Some will become mentally unstable after receiving great reports of treacherous activities within their own parliamentary groupings. We can only save the planet by exposing everyone who does not have the planets' interests in their own hearts. We cannot allow the treacherous actions to prolong the now last throws of the mother Earth's rebirth. In comparison you will also experience some leaders beginning to open up their own spiritual aspects. Not before time.

After this onslaught of hypocrisy and spiritual evolvement, another aspect will be revealed – that of spiritual hierarchy. We have not as yet made ourselves known directly to the governmental figures, but when the changes have been completed, we will allow some of the governmental figures to become aware of our presence. This will be carried out when the fracas is over and there is a new order possible. Everything comes to the man who waits, this patience period is now truly due to come to fruition.

After the onslaught of governmental suicides (we do not mean this to sound as if the physical act will be carried out, but only that they will destroy themselves on a mental and superiority level), the mainstay of the government will be completed by introducing those who are not at present involved in the actual government, but who for many years have been subscribing to the good of the planetary system. These may well be people who have never thought of themselves as political peoples, but who nevertheless have always thought of the good of the planet. The view must now be one of oneness not one of superiority of position within the grouping.

Our formula for success is guaranteed if the new government figures are primarily accounted for on a spiritual level. After the onslaught of governmental actions you will very quickly experience our powers. We cannot command a response, but as usual we will find the energy lines to enable us to command change. This is indirect action by us, but can only be carried out in this way to enable the cosmic consciousness to be raised. The raising of consciousness will prevent actions that could provoke more anger and bitterness to rise within the consciousness of the man in the street. We do not expect a medal to be given – only that the mainstream of consciousness be aligned with the universal mind. Our procedures are becoming much more acceptable, now that the escape plan will not in fact come into effect until every possible alternative route has been explored, and more to the point, activated. We bring you news and grievances, but as always come in love and faith that the plan will be successful.

Over a period of time there will be much to carry out on the political front. We do not insist that you become politically involved, but what we require is that you become politically aware. This will enable you to work within all fields of clearance. There is much to carry out within the political field. We will be challenging many to follow their spiritual paths, and also combine with the 'political' politicians. This will not be easy, as their minds do not wish to allow political dictates to overpower their spiritual needs, but as always it is possible to become spiritual in each area of the arena.

Before too long there will be many who will see their paths as connected to the spiritual and political arena. We do not wish to use separation techniques. It is only through complete integration of oneness that our completion programme will be activated. Many will come, few will be chosen. We are at liberty to comment here that there are still many who do not choose to follow our call. They have presented themselves, but not their souls. We cannot use those who will not surrender to the oneness. The oneness will survive many a strife, but not after the demolition of openness. We do not expect complete surrender from everyone, but we do need surrender from the main parties involved in the completion process. A margin of ninety percent has been effected which will hold the new energies into their positioning.

The 'twists and turns' of certain star-seeded individuals are causing concern. Remember always that when one is called, the call will sound at first as if the memory did not really recall the signal. Then as time passes, the memory will start to recall in greater detail the signals of eternity, and the energies will begin to rise above and beyond the normal functioning. As time progresses, then the information will become like second nature, as if you have known it always. Stepping outside this arena will then become very negative. We must adjust all of your programmes to enable you to become at one with the new energy.

23-29 January 1994
We have spoken to you earlier about the earthquake, hurricane and tidal wave situation. We must adjust any disturbances in the Earth's crust by attempting to regulate the proximity of the disturbances to the land masses that require the momentum of the energy to be kept clean. Any disturbances will be made clear to you beforehand. This way we can help any of the light-workers that are situated in those disaster areas. The landmasses that will be affected most are those in the southern hemisphere, those that are surrounded by the negative energy accumulation that was once Atlantis and Lemurian soil. We must adjust the conclave areas that may collapse completely if and when the large cataclysmic changes occur. It is better thought of as an escape plan, rather than now as the only way out of the Earth's dilemma.

Very quickly the energies of the once tormented areas will become cleansed. We expect the minor alterations to help hinder the need for great cataclysmic changes in the future. Apart from these areas we will be giving you the exact locations of the freezing districts. In doing so we will expect the disaster areas to become more a case of 'expectancy breeds preparation' and indeed 'consolidation of resources', both within the preceding times before the actual happenings and the time of expectancy. Much of what is about to occur has been expected by those involved with the New Age thinking, but we must now prepare others who do not as yet realise the enormity of the situation already upon your planet Earth.

Do not hesitate to contact the mainstream press outlets and media officials. Our information will become as much a part of the everyday news items as the official data that is publicised. Do not also hesitate to become more open with the information that will be given. The time has passed when we needed to prime your spoken words. The time has now come for you to be prepared to offer everything to those who are willing to listen.

We begin by approaching the areas of extreme energy transference. There are certain areas in the miraculous regions of Calcutta that require balancing. These areas are very much involved in the depravities of your society. It was not of their own making, but because of the attitude of the governmental systems that were governing these areas. But nevertheless the energy must now be released. This will be done within the next seven weeks. It will begin with an enormous release of energy in the southern area, followed by several smaller releases beginning in the far-reaching eastern region.

Another region which will see great changes is on the southern side of Japan. This will begin the great changes destined for this country over the next ten months. Both inland and at sea, the area in and around Japan will undergo drastic movements. This will be in the form of earthquakes and also great tidal waves, some which will completely obliterate the coastal areas. Much of the area will be consumed by water, and the mud and debris. Tokyo has before been approached by disaster. The disaster that is now approaching is one of great magnitude. It is one of greater calamity than will be expected, because of this we will give you specific details of damage that will be encountered. If you are aware of this, then details can be given to the world. We do not give you empty words; it is because of our love for your people that we are attempting to forewarn those of you who are able to respond. The damage around the coastal inlet areas will be greatest. The energy that needs to be released has accumulated in these inlets because of the energy transference on your planet today.

It is easy for us to release pockets of energy, but in doing so we are at liberty to say that much damage will occur. Our master plan will be presented in a way that clears the energy despite human beings, but as our love goes out to you, we will forewarn you and your fellow man. It has become apparent that many of the inlets in Japan are jeopardised by traumatic happenings. We can adjust the energy towards the ocean, but only when this is appropriate. It must be understood that many of the inlets are holding high negative energy levels. After May 1st the energy will begin to resurface along the eastern coast and thereafter will dissipate along the edges of the north-eastern coastal areas.

Apart from this information there will be much to write about on the calculations of tidal waves and earth trauma. This information will be very much needed for your scientists to readjust their machinery to become in tune with Mother Earth. They are not so much in tune as trying to understand her patterns: this will ultimately lead to much inaccuracy and miscalculation. It is not because of their lack of awareness, but because of their lack of sensibility; to sense is to understand. You will find that if they are aware of the information, their minds will begin to readjust to the sensory devices which are available within your world now.

By the end of the year the onslaught of clearance will be complete; the aftermath will not be clear. As with any prolonged action the energies become vibrant, they become almost active on a level of explosion. These energies will become more subdued, but not deadened, as time goes by. The energies will prevent the escape of power along the lines of depravity. It is not enough to prevent the negative from controlling, but we must also complete the patterns so that the new grid system does not become decadent again. Our process is one of depth and breadth. It must protect the planet in time to come.

As we approach the next millennium, energies will build along these new power lines in order to prevent a repeat of decadent behaviour. Many ideas have been given as to the process in hand, but few are understanding that this will not be repeated; it cannot. The energies that are building are ones of the highest.

February 1994
Before too long the energy buildup around the eastern coast of France will become explosive. This energy has been holding tight for many months. The release will be a very long one, one which will become very explosive to the regions around the Dordogne. The areas most affected will be around Montpellier and Marseilles, but after a period of about three months, this energy will release much of the energy already stored within the Dordogne valley. Around the Dordogne area are many underwater streams and springs. Much of the energy held into these water caverns will become very explosive when

exposed to more extreme sources of magnetic energy. After a while the springs themselves will erupt, causing much flooding and, of course, much chaos amongst the people. This area will be very nearly lost under water for as long as six months. We cannot estimate exactly, but would not wish to restrict this to less time at this point in time.

Qu: Are the streams and springs under the ground known about by the people there?
No, they are satisfied with the underground water they have, but do not question why, when other places are becoming dry and arid, their ground does not become so. It is one of those things where, what you do not know, you do not question and because these springs have never caused them any problems before, then they do not question whether they exist. They have existed for approximately 20,000 years. Before that, this land was itself waterlogged. It has become dry or workable since the last very dry and hot time on this planet which came about when the last storms blew across the whole of the planet.

It is now time to discuss the oncoming events within the area known to you as Khartoum. This area has many energies that are not now required for the Earth in her newly acquired state. Within the next six months the area will become a monsoon; by this we mean that much rainfall will appear as if by magic. This area does not have this sort of rainfall of which we are speaking. The people will become very shocked and also very morose. This will happen because of their somewhat narrow view of life. They will believe that it has happened as a punishment. This may be so, but not the punishment which they understand. It is because of the outpouring negative energy flow that this area must be cleansed, not because of the negativity of the people as a whole. Some of the people are well and truly aligned to the earth spirits, but others are somewhat decadent.

The area itself is negative because of ancient rites that were practised here many decades ago. It is not because of the current situation. We cannot alter the course of the karmic system. This karma has been built up for a very long time; it is only now being allowed to disperse. The dispersing of the old ancient energies will give clearance to this area. It will not become malevolent again. The rainfall will be fleeting, but because of the arid landscape, the water will collect in vast masses upon the land area. It will become waterlogged very quickly. In order to redress the balance, it will need to be drained artificially by means of large water holes. This will enable the area to maintain water for some time afterwards. We cannot ask you to forewarn these peoples, as there would be no response. They do not think too highly of the western world, only of their own highly superstitious nature. It is because of the world situation that we tell you of these outcomes.

You must become aware of the entirety of the plan that is being imparted upon your Earth planet. If we do not give you all of the information you will not begin to understand the wholeness of the plan. This wholeness is very important. It is not just a short term plan, but the plan for the next phase of the entire planet Earth. Do not be alarmed at the frequency with which the information will predict changes. It is these changes which are balancing Mother Earth. She does not need what you would call a 'spit and polish': she requires more a complete restoration. We cannot cover over any of the negative energy build-ups. These must be rebalanced through a thorough cleansing.

Chapter 6.

February 1994
It has been a long time between the generations that had obeyed the more spiritually-testing obligations and the more recent idea that this generation has complete control of its own destiny. We must now show you of the infamously low control that this generation has over itself. It is because of the low control that we have been obliged to command the actions of the coming years. We must now apply more power to the energy that lies around your planet so that the escapage of descent is not so great. What we are endeavouring to accomplish is the release of more direct energy resources to those who are able to handle them.

As time goes on we will redirect the entire power resources through to the main beam of the angel's head. This energy will be used to readjust the main beam of power around the angel's wings, then after some time lapse, we will readjust again to include the propulsion action of the lower part of the angel's body. We are using a metaphor here so that you become aware of the wholeness of the project. It is not because of individual people that we are assisting mastery, but because of the main body of the angel. This angel is the saving grace of the planet Earth. Without her we cannot carry out the ascension process en masse. Without those people who make up the angel we cannot complete the process. The evacuation plan, the escape plan, would then be required. Our angel is now semi-complete; she has one arm, one leg and one knee. Without her wings she will not fly; without her arms she will not ascend; without her legs she will not walk the Earth again. Do you understand, dear ones, we must have more direct action from those who have chosen long ago to be a part of this mission?

Do not feel guilty. We do not require your guilt; we do require your immediate action. Our programme cannot be completed until more mainbeam workers are in place. Our place is to cause the propulsion from which the angel will ascend. Ascension does not require you to surrender your souls, only surrender to your souls. Maybe an understanding of surrender is required. We do not require that you understand any of what we are saying to you – only that you surrender – but we are at liberty to complain here that many are not surrendering; they are only playing a new game. A game with new dice and new competitions.

The complication that now grows is to complete the onslaught of negative energies without wiping out the mainbeam workers who are not already active. We will require that more information is given much more quickly to those who require it. It is not for anyone to judge who requires it and who does not – for who of you would know a sleeping star-seed whilst they are still asleep? Do not attempt to classify who may be still heavily cloaked and who is not. Some of the main keys have not yet been activated; by this we mean that there are still keys which are waiting to be given. These keys will be given as soon as they are asked for, we cannot activate them for you. Part of this plan must be presented to you as tests. These tests are not yet complete; on completion the angel will ascend. After the completion of the tests and the completion of the 'angel' presence, then will come the time of strife and then a time of harmony and peace will reign over your planet.

Not for a hundred years will we come and reign with you on planet Earth. We cannot come until all of the strife is over. After ascension, or mastery of the chosen ones, the Earth will complete her cycle as you know it. It has been a cycle of misfortune and miscalculation of time and energy. Her next cycle is one of cataclysmic cleansing and re-balancing. She does not need to completely obliterate the earth mass, but requires that harmony is reached to enable her to 'live' within her own separate energy field, surrounded by reliable guardians and custodians.

It is imperative that her energy field is completely cleansed and that the Earth's crust has renewed its resources. This can now only come about through thorough cleansing, or fumigation as you would see it in your great industrial buildings. This fumigation has to be 100% to be efficient, does it not? One germ would begin the old cycle all over again. We cannot have 'bacteria' alive on the planet. Many are beginning to assume that ascension will bring about drastic changes almost immediately. It will not – these changes will only bring about drastic changes to those of you who choose to ascend. The next few years will be spent converting the old into the new, the New Age. It is only the beginning, my dear ones. We do not wish to shock, but we must not lead you astray either. Our wishes are that you now begin to appreciate the importance of engaging within a quest to ensure that all information is given to everyone. We are the guardians of the Christ consciousness – and we are now welcoming you all to join us, be with us always. We are here to assist your passage, safely, to these new horizons.

February 1994
As we approach the millennium, the energy build-up will be immense. This energy will be released. It is because of this immense build-up that the cataclysmic action will be activated. After 1995 the energy releases will no longer be activated from the energy field. It is after this date that the earth changes will occur. There will be much destruction and change upon the planet Earth. We cannot estimate now just how much change there will be, but we can tell you that it will be immense. After the transition, the energies will begin to subside.

This will then lead to the next stage of the major plan which is that the oceans and waterways will be cleared. This clearance will begin the last stages of the Earth's physical rebirth. The plan of action from this point is one of universal concern, not planetary. The universal energy system has no motion, no time and no space; it is operational because it just 'is'.

The planet Earth will begin to adjust to universal energy from the last quarter of 1996. This will allow us to begin to realign the Earth within the energy field of the planetary cosmos. Much of what will happen is not explainable at this point in time. It will not be for some time yet that any of you will be able to understand the workings of the universal energy system. It is not sustained from any source within your mental capacity. We will endeavour to speak further of this later on, but as yet can find no words that will give you the understanding that you require. Be content now to operate with the knowledge that you do have and do understand.

There is much to do within the areas of which we have spoken. Know that after the transition has ended at the beginning of 1997, you will be very much altered in your states of mind. You will require no understanding; you will know and experience so much more. We have no hopes of endeavouring to open your minds at this point in time to the ultimate details of our plan. We can only trust that all will go to plan, both on a humanitarian level, as well as a planetary level. Before too long you will be expecting to know what is going to happen and when. We will arrange that you have all of this information.

This is Kuthumi, Hilarion, Gabriel and Raphael, gathered together in order to give you the peace, hope, faith and charity for all of the tasks that are left to be accomplished. We leave you with this message: Be not afraid of the oncoming changes. They are not so much changes, as innovations to bring about peace on Earth, which we know is your desire.

We begin today by allowing you to understand the outcome of the teachings that we have been giving you over the past three years. You must now understand the reason why we have made so much contact with you. We need now to allow you to give our words to many more people. Do not now approach this as information just for yourself. We have a need of your mind and your presence to convey to many more people the information that will be given to you. For some time now the information has been somewhat erratic. By this we mean that we have not followed a set, rigid format, when dictating these notes to you. From this time onwards we will be endeavouring to list the information in order of importance. By this we mean that there is an order of preference. This preference is only connected to the importance of what needs to be given, when. It is not only for our own usage. It is for the people that we need, to interpret which information needs to be heard and when.

By June this year you will be given a complete synopsis of the events to take place before the turn of the century. This first synopsis will be somewhat condensed. Then we will begin to give you more detailed information of each individual event. Each event will be logged in a synopsis which must be given to the public. This synopsis will be called the 'Advent Calendar'. By this we mean that each event is significant and an important part of the preceding events leading to the ascension of the planet Earth.

By March of next year all events will be exposed. This exposure will be forewarning for all those who have the ears to listen. We cannot now be responsible for those human beings who choose not to listen. If we do not warn them, then we could be held responsible.

The mission that you have undertaken is not an easy one. The masses of society will not want to listen. They will only listen when goaded on by the impulses of hypocrisy. Those who do listen will be heralded as insane – or much worse – criminals. The mission that you have chosen so long ago was one that would implicate you in the task of allowing those who can 'hear' to have confirmation in a firm and logical format, so that their faith does not wane as things become more and more difficult within the Third dimension. It is because of this action that strength will be built up within the quarters of the population that are waking up. We must have sustained strength within the enlightened ones.

You have chosen to become part of the backbone of this shoring-up process. At every crossroads there is always self-doubt and nervousness of action. As the crossroads are presented we need those on the pathway to feel sure that they can walk boldly on, knowing that all is well on the cosmic pathway. As each crossroad is presented, the information that you will be given will assist those who begin to doubt the cataclysmic actions around them as being correct. This Advent Calendar will become part of the information relied upon to estimate how far you have progressed with the evolvement of Mother Earth towards ascension, and also how far there is left to go.

All of this information will be daunting. We do not expect you to become emotionally involved in the sequence of events, only involved in doing what must be done.

We will begin today by giving you the title, and also an agenda of events:

ADVENT CALENDAR FOR THE SALVATION OF THE PLANET EARTH
These events will progress concurrently as given:

Book II.
Part 1: Spring cleaning the areas of the planet Earth that have accumulated negative energy.

Part 2: Massive shifts in the Earth's crust that will enable much of the energy caught beneath the surface to release.

Part 3: The beginning of the cleansing of the oceans and waterways.

Part 4: The passing of the Sun in front of/between the Moon and the stars.

Book III. *[This is in the process of being channelled]*
Part 1: The operating of the universal energy system incorporating planet Earth.

Part 2: The completion of the universal energy system continuum.

Part 3: Ascension for the planet Earth.

Part 4: Holy Order.

The fourth book will not be logged for some time, as your understanding and expectancies will cloud the information, and clarity will not reign.

Each section of the calendar will be given separately, so that it is read in sections. This will enable much of the information to be given without causing any confusion, and subsequent misunderstandings. You will assist us greatly if you are able to comprehend the enormity of this process. We must have your sworn oath of allegiance to the planet Earth and her Creator's progress for her.

We thank you, and remain true to our allegiance to the Mother Earth in her time of great change. We are always your counterparts on the celestial planes. We come as angels bearing great gifts of knowledge to those willing to listen.

Master Kuthumi, Master Hilarion and Archangel Gabriel. (8th February 1994)

BOOK TWO

Advent Calendar for the Salvation of the Planet Earth

Channelled February to May 1994

PART ONE

Chapter 7.

The Spring Cleaning of the Planet Earth

February 1994

At this moment in time, the Earth has become severely damaged by humanoid existence. She does not stand easy in her orbit. We must attempt to cleanse the areas that have for so long harboured negative energy. The cleansing will begin with the 'dirt' being stripped from the energy lines. This will commence when the energy that has been placed upon the Earth reaches its highest frequency. We cannot give a date for this, because there are many factors that affect the energy reaching its highest frequency. The frequency at the moment has reached the fifty percent mark, and is in the process of rising again. From this time on, the energy will rise in increments of about ten percent. This will enable the population to begin to realise what is happening, rather than be shocked into submission. We are awaiting the time when the energy reaches approximately seventy-five percent before the preparation for the cleansing can begin.

This preparation will begin with much upheaval in the areas of the main energy lines. The main energy lines are the ones which govern the fast reactor system of lines. By this we mean that the system will only begin to cleanse when the major lines are activated. Then the minor ones will carry out their own cleansing process. After the major lines have been activated, there will be much change concerning the areas in which they are situated. Much of this change will involve ironing out the problems of food and water. Because of the activation the areas will become very problematic concerning cultivation, and much worse, water supply. The energy itself will be of a much higher frequency, which will in turn affect the land and drainage.

Much of the land will need to be cleared of old crops and old water or drainage systems. After the energising of the core centres, the energy will swell the lines, causing breakup of the soil and subsoil, and much will be lost through the pervading energy release. This does not entail earth movement within the interior or between the plates, but much more superficial movement. We call this superficial to enable you to gain perspective of what we call real shifts and energy releases.

Much of this movement will be concerned with the areas around Scotland, Majorca, Tunisia, the Spanish mainland, Italy, Nova Scotia, and Portland in Oregon. These particular areas are in much need of cleansing. It is not because of the people now inhabiting the land, but because of the past history. It will be considered as part of the bad luck of the draw as it were, because nobody at this point will consider that there are major energy shifts and interference affecting the land itself.

Do not be too concerned with these effects. They will not cause too much affray, but will need to be counted as the beginning of the more major cleansing actions. After these lines have been correctly charged, you will begin to see other surrounding areas become more adaptable to the new changing climates. Around the Spanish mainland there will be new growth beginning to emerge in the way of fresh, greener grasslands and more interesting species of plant life. This will give way to lush crops and more exotic undergrowth. In Tunisia the soil will become more friable, and eventually much more of an economically viable cultivation area.

In Scotland, much of the land will be lost to sea, but before this begins energy will be felt around the Highlands to such an extent that one will believe the heavenly hosts have descended. This will cause many to leave the area, but also to invade. It will be entirely dependent upon the vibration of those concerned. It is a major cleansing in Scotland, one which she will never recover from. Scotland, as you know it, will not be in existence for much more than three years. After this period of time the area will become partly waterlogged and partially extinct. The waves will wash upon the Scottish shores for more than three months with a wind velocity that has never been felt on your planet before, and will never be felt again. Much of the Scottish coastline will be lost. There are few areas which will remain, but these are much further southward, and extending into England. The smaller islands will not survive; they have for a long time lived on borrowed time – this time was allowed because of the upgrading consciousness of the people now inhabiting the islands. Much of the land that will be lost will remain deep below the ocean. Smaller pieces of land will appear to the west of the Hebrides; these pieces of land will become inhabited only by small wildlife.

Nova Scotia has many inlets and islands. Much of the land within these inlet areas will become waterlogged and then extinct. It is because of the negative energies that lay around these inlets that much of the land will be lost. If the energy is only slightly negative, then land is not lost, but just rebalanced. If the energy has accumulated debris within its field, then it cannot be rebalanced, but must be rejected.

Much of the land within the area known to you as the Hebrides will become rejected. Other far northern areas of Scotland have much debris lodged within the energy system. We cannot readjust these energies; they must be finally and completely rebalanced. After rebalancing, the land will be lost; it will not recover.

Much of the land around the Nova Scotia inlets will be released into the ocean. This is because of the energy build-up and firmly entrenched lumps of negative debris in the energy field.

After balancing, any energy that has not been cleansed is released into the ocean, together with landmass attached to it. At a later stage, the oceans themselves will be completely cleansed of this negative energy, but first we must cleanse the earth areas. If we do not cleanse the earth areas first, then the oceans will not be able to filter the energy debris. We cannot lose earth matter. We must enable the Earth's filter system to include all debris.

The Earth is complete in herself; she does not lose or gain anything during any of the civilisations on Earth, only cleanses and rebuilds. If she was not inhabited, then she would be self-cleansing constantly in order to stay clean. It is only because of the human involvement that her system has become severely clogged. Your energies are an intrusion on the Earth planet. It was only because of divine intervention that humans were allowed to inhabit the Earth plane.

Much of the cleansing will be carried out through the Earth's own system. If we require more 'cleansing fluids', then we will be allowed to use surges of energy. These surges will be in the form of storm blasts. Storm blasts are quick, calculated blasts of electric energy which may devastate areas, but will nevertheless cleanse any debris and negative vibrations. We do not wish to harm, therefore these will only be used as a last resort.

Portland has much negative energy within the land mass of this city. This has been caused by too much pontificating over environmental issues. These discussions have concentrated energy around the coastal area, causing negative build-up. Much of the discussions have been proposing excuses as to why nothing has been accomplished in the way of environmental issues. The Portland area has much pollution. This has been caused by too much waste and not enough positive action to dissolve the piles of rubbish that are awaiting destruction.

There are many reasons why certain areas have accumulated negative stockpiles of energy. Firstly, energy is maintained in certain areas because of negative thought. These negative thoughts can be of different substance; some are just plain negative areas where for many centuries the attitudes of the people have been negatively inclined. Other areas are negative because of past action of the people inhabiting them as in the case of wars and military action. These areas require much scrubbing and sterilising because of the thought patterns of the oppressors and the oppressed. The most difficult areas to deal with are those that have suffered poverty and sickness. These areas accrue much waste within the fine lines of the energy system. These fine lines have to be cauterised in order to change the energy flow to positive.

We have many different methods of dealing with negative energy, both air and water are weapons against this polluted energy supply, but of course the air must be propelled by fast action, and the water would need to be immense; hence why we use the system of the weather to help us with our task. These weather changes are not just a random event happening because of the change in energy on the planet. They are part of the overall plan.

We must attempt to clean some of the unwanted energies before the earth changes take place. If the earth changes take place before the energy has been somewhat cleansed, then the action will be doubly traumatic. We do not talk in jest. We must have your attention as to why these changes will take place. All the pieces of the jigsaw must be in place by the turn of the century. If they were not, then the Earth planet would be obliterated. The energy system is not just one of fine alignment; it is the life source of not only the planet Earth, but all people who populate her.

We cannot speak strong enough words to warn you that every thought that is presented on the planet Earth must be positive. You are responsible for her welfare and also your own survival. Negative thoughts propel negative actions, both in mankind and on an energy level. Many of you will wonder how this can be. We will try to give you an example which will simplify this for you. If a man tries to give instructions to a dog that he requires to go to another place; if he continually instructs the dog, but points in another direction, the dog will most certainly be confused and most probably will go towards the direction that he points. If you continually state that you want peace and harmony, but go on projecting out negative thoughts, then negativity is what you get.

We must have no more confusion. We will cleanse the planet, but she must stay clean. This in not now an option; those who cannot stay in a positive frame of mind will not survive in the energies that are upgrading on your planet. We do not speak of months; but over the next few years it will become increasingly more and more difficult to sustain life from a lower vibrational frequency.

The next stage of the cleansing process will involve the areas of Greece – mainland and islands. She will become very much involved in strife as the energy system in that part of the world is quickened. Much of her strife will be connected with the energy lines which run from the edge of the continent to the island of Majorca. The island of Majorca will take the main part of the energy input, but as she is connected to Greece both by energy lines and inheritance, then she will be very badly affected. The effects will be somewhat of a different nature, as she has much rock formation, both on the surface and beneath the ocean around her coastline; this rock formation will be affected greatly. The land areas themselves will become somewhat concertinaed, meaning that they will suffer somewhat of a jarred affect. This will cause much land to be lost, but not necessarily great loss of life, as this country is not greatly populated.

We must now attempt to address the problems which lie within the West Indies. This area has much confusion, both on an energy level and within the land masses themselves. We do not consider that the area is polluted, but much has been laid down within the energy field. This has a lot to do with the overall energy of the people. They have somewhat of a casual nature – one that does not promote action. They must be given the instructions to become more warrior-like. We do not mean aggressive, but low-key optimism. We need to adjust their environment so that the energy holds more fire vibration. By this we mean energy that is actually inspiring and creative – both in a warrior-like way and passive. It is of no use to hold the passive way all of the time. They must enrich their characters and become spiritual warriors. Very soon the energy around this area will become fired up. We will create this energy by earthquake and volcanic eruptions. We do not need to create the energy to bursting point, but just enough to point them in the correct direction. The direction they are going is somewhat decadent because of the lack of energy. They are much more involved with pleasure than spiritual practices. The energy from the earthquakes will involve them in survival which will instil in them the energy needed.

We do not hesitate to quicken the energy when it is needed, but we will not destroy. Destruction will only come if our call is not answered by the turn of the century. Every one of you will hear the call. It will come in a myriad of ways, but will always be the call of the Divine. Our ability to adjust energies is one that will save the planet. We have no conscience over this matter. Our ability will become your ability when you have completed your pathways. We come as friends, not foe. We do not endanger. You only come to serve the needs of the time ahead. It is our ability which will guide you to the higher planes.

It is very important that you all have the understanding as to why these exchanges will take place. We must add here that it is not because of the people; it is because of the planet Earth. Much movement happens within the universal system. It is not obvious to you on planet Earth with your Third dimensional understanding. It is only because of the oncoming changes that you will become involved.

Our main information is given in order for you to align with the universal energy system. It is a way of conveying to you the enormity of the task ahead for mankind. Mankind will survive, but will become very much more in line with the other universal beings. Mankind has become severely backward in his attempts for growth within the solar system. He has become very involved in attempting to understand the logic of the Universe, but not the spiritual understanding.

The universal energy system cannot be understood from purely a logical point of view. It is only when man becomes spiritual first and foremost that he will even begin to understand the workings of the universal energy. Much has been accomplished within technology and science, but this will not help you now.

The next decade must bring about the spiritual revolution that is needed to rebalance the energies of mankind. We cannot stress enough the need for spiritual rebalancing. This does not require much effort, only Divine inspiration being received dutifully upon the Earth. This duty is one that is owed to yourselves and your creators. Before too long you will feel the pull towards the mainstream universal energy system. It is because of this that the spiritual revolution will commence. This pull will begin when the energies upon your planet are up-graded to the seventy-five percent originally mentioned. Until that point we can only adjust those who are already willingly awakening.

This universal energy will indicate to you how vast this system is. It does not cover just your solar system. It is involved in numerous solar systems, some that you are not even aware of. It covers the whole of the cosmic solar system. It will be beyond your comprehension at this point to consider how large this is. It is as if you were just a pin prick in the middle of a vast map that does not end. We will continue now with the events that will precede the large earth movements within your planet Earth.

Before the beginning of the year 1995 the energy around the Atlantic Ocean will become very torrid. This will lead to much land loss in the areas of Sweden and Denmark. The Atlantic Ocean will become over-swelled and cause great tidal waves upon the beaches of both these countries. It is because of the build-up of energy within the middle of the Atlantic that this will occur. The North Sea will become exceptionally over-full, and cause great changes along the coastlines of these countries. You do not understand yet how these oceans interconnect on an energy level; when one is under stress, the others respond. It is as if they are part of the same entity, which undoubtedly they are. The oceans have one energy – that of the element of water. It does not matter where the trouble begins, all will feel it.

This build-up of energy will also cause much of the coastline of France to be affected. She will suffer much loss of life as her coastal areas are not well protected. Most countries have managed to prepare in some way for changes that may occur; France has not.

This build-up will also affect some parts of Northern Canada. Around the areas of the Great Lakes the energy will become torrid. The Great Lakes will become affected because of streamline energy transference. Below the lakes are energy lines which join with the energy of the Atlantic Ocean and the Pacific Ocean. Because you cannot see these energy lines below the oceans, you have not really taken them into account. Much is said of the energy lines within the earth areas, but not so of the oceans.

We must adjust your understanding to cover all aspects of the planet Earth. Before too long you will see how her digestive system works. It has a liver and gall bladder just as you have. These organs will adjust the energy by digesting anything that is not of use. Below the oceans are many energy lines. These play an important part in the energy of the planet. You must now consider that the planet Earth is a complete organism. After much stress she must cleanse and recover. The recovery period will come at the end of the millennium.

We can give you a complete diagram of the energy system of the planet; this will enable you to see for yourselves the connections between one place and another. It will assist you in understanding how the cleansing will take place. The energy lines themselves are circular; they have no beginning and no end. This is why when action is taken in one area, it affects another, be it ever so far away. What goes out comes back to the beginning; until these lines are clear – then the action goes on repeating itself. Because of the interference on these lines, we need to adjust the main energy points. Along each line are a number of what we would call transformers. These transformers act to meter out the energy along the line. If the transformer itself becomes clogged, then the line is almost out of control. Any energy can travel along the line without being metered. The cleansing process will continue until each one of these lines is clean – then the new energy can be released full blast. Until this time you must expect that things will be very traumatic. You yourselves can visualise this cleansing process taking place. It is not something to fear; it is something to celebrate. Do not try to abate this process, for all will be lost.

Italy will become lost to the sea for a time. Her neighbouring countries will assist her at this time. Much of the energy around Italy has become dirtied by the administration of negative attitudes. The sea around her coastlines will swell and cover much of her topsoil. She will recover very well because of the attitude of the people. They will join together to recover the land. The water will seep away after approximately twelve months. The land that was before very arid will become lush and productive. Much will need to be done to cleanse the oceans of the debris collected from the land masses, but we will assist you with this as the time approaches.

The cleansing will continue with much landsliding and energising of land masses. Amongst those areas to suffer greatly will be those of Sweden and Mesopotamia. Mesopotamia has many mountains and streams. These will become loose and muddy, causing much slipping of the land into the sea. These mountains have become covered by topsoil. They have been covered over during other great periods of cataclysm on the Earth planet. The mountains are now harbouring great energy forces. They are built of rock and granite, and have held energy for many generations. The area which joins the sea has an escape valve which feeds the energy to other parts of the world.

The areas around Mesopotamia will feed energy to various other countries. When we energise one particular place, it will affect many others. You cannot have an energy system that just responds in one particular area. The word system enables you to understand the complexity of what is about to come to pass. Sweden herself will recover, but not for a great many years. She will be habitable, but not on the scale of today. Her masses of population will leave before the energising has been completed.

Many will flee these areas because of non-understanding of events. It is because of this that we must try to allow as many people as possible to understand. Before long these events will become day-to-day events. Your newsrooms will not be able to keep ahead of the information being thrown on their desks.

Chapter 8.

Before too long there will be a lot of confusion from the media when certain events are explained in a compromising way. It is not because of the media personnel themselves, but because of the standards of conduct from the heads of the press agencies. They do not understand that press comments should be built on a purely logical, analytical basis; that the people at large should be given their own freedom to adjust their own feelings to the events that are beginning to happen around the planet. We cannot adjust the way that the events will be reported, but we can attempt to infiltrate into the sections of the media which will allow this. We will be using certain star-seeded individuals to attempt to address these media circuits.

On a scale of judgment, we will be addressing those of you who are willing to sacrifice the mantle of deliberation of attitude for the self-sacrificing mantle of spiritual reform. We have reasons beyond your comprehension of thought in offering this exercise to those who can go beyond their own personal desires and needs, and now walk the path naked of self-distortion. Apart from the media circuits, we will be attempting to secure places on every platform of every country, in order to allow all of the information to be given out to every individual willing to listen. Before too long the long-awaited events of cleansing will begin to adjust, around the perimeters of the Earth's crust. This will enable much more of the catalytic programme to become activated.

We do not expect all of you to be occupied in a direct manner with these catalytic events. There are many vocations for the star-seeded ones. These will include much addressing of the nations, much cleansing of the energy lines, much duplication of occupations, in order for the events to become known throughout the quarters of the Earth occupied by mankind. Many of you will become involved in several different areas of innovation. This will be because of certain factors now present within your characteristics of personality. Do not attempt to adjust any of the dials of your encoded systems. The coded dials are correct, well-adjusted and ready to activate with every burst of energy vibration presented towards the energy field of your planet.

As time goes by you will see that the words we speak are not empty. Each word is well chosen in order to give you much pre-warning of certain doubts and misjudgements that you may experience along this treacherous path. We have chosen well our word of treachery. Treachery is a state of being that each one of you knows well. Do not attempt to understand why or how this word will present itself to you in the future, but become aware of the enormity of the occupational risks that each one of you will encounter.

After much discussion and arguing, many of the politicians awaiting guidance from the central system will begin to discuss other means, other ways of guiding the country. The only argument that they will be in agreement with is the one of 'nothing happens without the knowledge of mastery and intent'. To begin with, the arguments will not centre around the issues currently escaping from the media mouthpieces, but will centre around issues of courage and fortitude of action, that although addressed in the past have never become actioned and therefore cases of reform. There will much debating issues of power and neglect, issues which have long become lost and adulterated. It is only through the realisation that people now expect politicans to become the people that they instructed their press personnel to personify in their manifestos, that will clear any of the negativity from the political parties.

The political front, or gateway as we would call it, will readjust and rectify many of the expectancy areas that the public will respond to; but alas these will be wasted, as great changes occur within the landmasses around both the United Kingdom and Russia. The arguments will end; much disaster will quell the energy being used in this fashion. As disaster creates disaster, each political party will address only the issues of survival – not change, or administering government from a humanitarian perspective. We cannot adjust these events; the changes that will be spoken of here will come, but not until a good period of time has elapsed.

The next three years will become as if Hell has become unleashed upon the earth plane. It is not Hell, but you will hear these words spoken by those who have not adapted to the oncoming energy transferences. We have spoken many times of those who will survive the apocalypse, and those who will not have the ability to come to terms with these times of grace. Grace is not widely acceptable to your peoples. They are in fear of an all-punishing godhead. They cannot begin to adjust to spiritual waves of energy, nor the appearance of a hierarchy coming in peace and love. There is a twist in the terms of conduct; the twist is one of complete surrender. The surrender of which we speak comes easily when one has become enlightened. When one only sees through the eyes of darkness, surrender would be the ultimate blow of death. Surrender has many side issues, the most despicable to the people in power is that of loss of 'face'.

It will come to pass that much of the energy releasing into the oceans will become bleak or blackened; much damage will occur to the marine life over a period of ten months. Because of the death toll within the ocean, much debris will accumulate and cause more problems. The rivers and waterways will also concentrate into dark, dank waters. We do not anticipate complete pollution of all waterways, but there will not be many that do not suffer in some way. Much of the ocean will be polluted, but this will be dealt with at a later point in time. We require that you begin to understand how and why these events will take place. Much has been addressed on pollution, but we require you to understand how this comes about.

The problem is not physical, but to do with energy. Much of your planet has become polluted by energy disturbances. It is not enough to cleanse the physical, as it is not enough to dress yourselves in smart clothes. It is what is being affected from an energy level that counts. You cannot make a silk purse from a sow's ear! If the finery is not present at the core of the person then the energy will be 'dirty'. It is the same with your planet Earth. She cannot be held in a dirtied energy field and be expected to perform to her ultimate qualities.

The core of the Earth is pure, as are all individuals, but these qualities of purity cannot be allowed to operate through a dirty energy field. It is three-fold: the energy, the physical and the outer persona. When the outer persona controls the inner core, then we have duality, when the inner controls the outer we have beauty and oneness. The Earth cannot control her outer without the help of the parasites who live upon her. She must be allowed to stabilise her resources, this way she will come back to her pure state, free of impurities and her energy field will flow free again.

Much of what has become negative is connected with the monstrosities that man has become involved with. Much of the nuclear power objectives are damaging the auric field around the planet; the energies are conflicting with the soft, sensuous energies of your Mother Earth. The word 'nuclear' has many connotations. It is considered to be a great invention, but we would beg to differ. The word itself can be broken down into new ideas – non-completion, benefits outcast and broken promises.

These broken promises will be amounting on a system of revenge, the revenge will be from the Earth to her guardians. Do not be surprised when she repays you in full. This system will be broken down in two ways: one that she will pay her debts to you for the custodianship that has been well fulfilled, and the other is of a debt owed to her. Be aware of the debts that you personally owe, do not try to evade any of these, you are both martyrs and eating humble pie. We will be responding now to your debts: you can allow these to be balanced when you respect our plan and our advice.

For some time now the energy of the Earth herself has been somewhat 'smogged'. As your system of understanding terminology is limited only to the areas that you have deemed important, then we must re-invent words to qualify our meaning. This 'smogging' has very nearly suffocated the energy system that controls the 'respiratory' process of Mother Earth. She cannot breathe, she cannot yawn, she cannot sing. She must now recover her breath or die for ever. This would never be allowed; her breath is a part of the breath of the universal energy system. It is through Mother Earth that the galactic energies are accumulating into the explosive suns. We are forever tripped up by the lack of understanding that you have of the universal energy system. Do you not wonder how this planet has been kept 'alive'. Do you not consider that if she was not alive, then none of you would be alive also? We are agasp at the ignorance that still holds mankind into a deep and unconscious sleep. Maybe this coma has had its period of incubation and the chrysalis will emerge with its new colours and new wings to fly. We breathe with you and on you in order to awaken you.

Be at ease with these words. We must feed you new energies, new light and love in order to awaken those sleepy eyes that you have kept closed for so long. Be not afraid of these comments, when you are awakened you will rejoice with us in the New Age and the new-found peace that will await you there. During this period of trauma and catastrophic happenings we will bring to you many gifts. These gifts will enable you to keep surviving through until the period of peace and happiness. Many of you now await your gifts. You are already in anticipation of how you will be able to help others, and also assist your own passage through to the real New Age.

We will not keep you waiting long; much of the stewardship has passed – you will become masters. Much of the time recently has been taken up with awarding merits to those of you who have waited by the side of this road. You have played your parts, but not as some in the mainstream. You have travelled the road much on your own and have not wanted acclaim or fortitude from the masses. We have now assisted you forward and can adjust the blueprint to bring about the clearance that is needed to expand your energy fields, in order for ascension to take place.

This ascension process has been very much misunderstood. We have meanings which do not resonate with your terminology and therefore we have adjusted our wording to correspond to any termi-nology that can be used. We do not treat this lightly. We are aware of the misdirections that have been given, but we must deal with you as best we can. We are dealing with sleepy heads who cannot answer our true callings to them. The birds do not answer if the call is not from one of their own grouping. We have adjusted our calling in order to grant some semblance of an answer. At a later stage you will hear our true call, you will answer, you will join with us in calling others.

Make sure that you have adjusted your own codings to respond when we call. If your dials are not centred on the right station, then you will hear other callers! Your dials when positioned correctly will resonate clearly and powerfully any of our messages; do not allow interference to be clearer than us. In order to reposition your dials, then correct any of the procedures which take you away from your spiritual mantle, you must now align every area of your lives with your true spiritual self. It is not enough to correct just the obvious roadways; you must cleanse and purify all of the areas of your life.

Do not try to avoid particular issues because of what others might feel, if you feel it needs to be cleansed, then it does. Do away with mistrust and negligence. Negligence will not support you when you need to be exact with your own survival. If you are at the mercy of others, you will not be able to read the signs as they are given. The signs will be crystal clear, but so must the eyes to see them. Any clouding of your own vision through emotional dependence will not make it easy for you to see.

Every individual on this planet must be able to see their own pathway. There are no joint pathways, only pathways that intertwine and twist with others, but not always linked not always dual pathways or even triple. Many of you would have us create massive 'freeways' so that you can amble along these in your hundreds, like packs of wolves. We have no wish to disturb you, but you must see the humour in what we perceive as we watch over you. Many are hoarding together now before the transition. They are not willing to step out alone and confront their own pathways. So we have many packs of wolves that must be dispersed.

Do not travel in packs; packs can only control themselves through group consciousness. They eat, they sleep and they make waves for others. We do not require you to create waves. We require you to create the need for others to follow our ways, not yours. This will come about much more quickly by following the law of the one. The law of the one is to become as closely affiliated to your own higher self. In time others will be spun around by the higher energies that you hold within your own energy field. Words will not be needed, only justice of mind and thought.

Have you never considered why the energies of Jesus Christ did not need to be thought-processed? He was not a great speaker; he was complete in his over-self. The people who came to him did not need to listen to the words, they were healed on receiving the energy of the master himself. It is not widely thought of as miracles, but when one person is linked to another by pure energy transference, then the energy present is of the Christ consciousness. It is possible at that moment for complete healing of the mind, body and spirit, but as usual the mind will question the act as soon as it has begun. This is because the mind at this moment in time will not surrender.

When our cycle of cleansing is over, it will be possible to heal by thought transference. The energy around the planet will hold more of the Christ consciousness on a more direct level. This will enable many more of you to complete the healing process for yourselves and then for others. Your spirits will become as birds soaring higher and higher as the 'smog' is cleared. The energy present will be of a calibre that has not been known on the planet Earth since her beginning.

Very soon much energy will release next to the spring equinox energy. Many of you are aware of the energies released around springtime. This time the energy will be complimented by extreme energy transference in the form of dust and particles of extreme light interference. Brilliant light will accompany your springtime, this light does not come from the Sun, but from the areas of the solar system that are at present unknown to you. We hesitate to give you more details at present, because of the unknown factors that you will consider adrift from the scientific and astronomical factors known.

Be at ease with these words. It is important that you begin to understand that many of your peoples have bamboozled you into believing untruths. These untruths will be discovered later, but we will endeavour to give you now some of the effects of the lightening energies that will descend upon the planet Earth. The effects will be somewhat catastrophic when the energies reach the summer equinox. Many will fear for their lives as energies unleash many of the toxic wastes that have been stored. These toxic wastes will react to the energies that descend. They have not been neutralised; only contaminated with more chemicals that will themselves respond to the new enlivened energy forms.

Much disaster will ensue in areas that are already alight with negativity. These areas lie around the areas of desert, and danger zones where nuclear explosions have been performed. The negativity surrounding these particular areas is extreme. Do not be taken in by the reports that issue safety factors. There can be no safety in these areas for many years. After the onslaught of negative release, these areas will be barren and therefore uninhabitable. We will assist the cleansing of these areas at a later stage, but for now they should remain empty and closed off from all human habitation. Much will be said when we begin the energy clearance, but as usual much will be misinterpreted.

Chapter 9.

We are present amongst you in order to give warnings of the coming changes. The events that will come to pass have been calculated for many years. These events will bring about the necessary dilemmas that will ensure that you will again return 'home'. This home is the home that you remember, the home that you miss, the home that you so wish to return to. We cannot be responsible for those who do not wish to put in the effort required in order to make this homeward journey. This journey is one that should not be missed; it is within this journey that you will again meet with those friends that you have not been with for many lifetimes. It is the journey that will enable you to complete your mission. The only mission that was presented in the beginning of 'time' was the one of return. It is through answering the calling now that you will begin this journey home. We cannot answer for you. We will give the call many more times before the ultimate changes occur; but as has been destined – we will call, but are unable to take control of you and pull you into line.

There will be many who will not hear us calling. They will wait until their screams will be heard echoing amongst the debris, echoing in desperation as the beginning of the end of Third dimensional existence begins. Their cries will be echoed amongst the dead, the living and the evolved. There will be many who will not be there when the end is hallowed. Begin now to discriminate between the levels of evolution, between the energies of those that are with you, those that are against you and those that will be influenced by you. It is only time that will evolve these answers for you. We cannot be your judge and jury; you must begin to address these questions in order to protect yourselves and those that you guide.

When the energies become 'peaked' we will begin to cleanse each country, each ocean and every avenue that holds the power of negativity. Before the great cataclysmic oceanic waves begin to rise there will be many who will discuss the answers to the problems that beset your planet. These questions and indeed answers will not give solutions. We cannot compete with the monstrosities that have been performed upon planet Earth. We must cleanse. Much discussion will only bring more grief, there are no explanations that can be given when one does not consider the overall plan of the cosmic energy system.

We begin now to offer you the understandings that you require, but first we must endeavour to protect some of the areas that are in most need. These areas are the areas that will become New Age settlements. There will be many of these settlements that will come into being; some are destined, some will be 'man' made. There will be many who gather together in fear. The areas that are protected will be for those that gather in harmonious peace and continuum. The protection that will be offered will be much to do with energy, the energy that is already present in the earth areas that contain uranium. This energy is convulsive; it requires energising, but does not require storage or contamination. It will be utilised on a higher level by those individuals who are now evolving into their light bodies. Uranium has been coveted in the past and contaminated. We will now show you how it can be captured and utilised with the energy of the Sun. The Sun will activate uranium and shower you with energies of protection.

Much of the area known to you as Spain contains minute deposits of uranium. Because of this we will be giving you exact locations within the Spanish mainland that hold these secret deposits. Many of the land areas within the area known to you as Croatia have deposits of uranium. The land that lies east and west of the Suez canal contains deposits of uranium mixed with deposits of iron ore. This iron ore deposit does not have the same qualities as the deposits that are at present used within the world economy system. It is iron ore, but without the veins of metallic content. It is used mainly as a consolidating material for bricks and mortar. It should not be used in this way; it contains minute particles of uranium, and will attract extremely dangerous energies within the households and business properties that it is used in.

Before too long your scientists will be testing many more substances as they begin to realise that their knowledge up to this time has not been particularly enlightened. Because of the time factors involved here in the onslaught of negative energy release, it will be too late for you to receive information from the scientists – they are behind time. We will be giving you information that can be given to scientific institutions in order for them to prepare the way now for a lot of the old rules of thumb to be changed. They will have their eyes opened once and for all. It will be as if they have removed the blinkers, or rather that the blinkers have been ripped away.

Many of your scientists operate from the stance that 'everything comes to the man that waits'. Well, it does, if the man is still around to receive it, but in the coming two years there will be many that do not remain upon this planet, and therefore the waiting will be in vain. We do not jest. We cannot warn you enough of the onslaught of negative energy release. You have built these energies – you must now experience their release. Do not be disappointed if we do not give all the information to you at one time. We temper in order to avoid shock waves. We cannot give you large amounts of information that will then put you into a state of numbness. We will provide you with as much information as you can digest at one time. Bit by bit, you will begin to enter into our world and with a closer examination of your own.

Around about June of this year the energy will be holding sufficient condensed particles of higher vibration to cause much releasing. This releasing will occur in the areas of Scotland, Nova Scotia, Sweden and Norway. The areas of Majorca, Italy and Tunisia will begin to cleanse very shortly afterwards. It is because of the main energy line activation that this release will be felt. This main line begins in Nova Scotia and ends in the far western regions of Mesopotamia. It is because of this line that Scotland will be affected, and also the areas of Sweden and Norway. Many peoples will also be affected.

We cannot protect every person on every piece of mainland – it is impossible. Those that feel the energies will leave these places before the release. In many places, just before the releasing takes place, many will feel high heavenly host energies. This is connected with the energy with which we will be activating the lines. This energy can be felt along the lines as they are activated. It will not be there for very long, but as soon as this is felt, the releasing will have started. It will build from a slow beginning to a vast crescendo. This feeling of activation can be used as a marker to assist you with what is happening around the globe.

We will be activating many lines at different times. There will be intervals in between, but as soon as one line has completed, we will activate the next. You will have a succession of buildups and explosive releases. As soon as one completes the next begins, as if we were choreographing a show. We do not expect you to applaud, but be aware of the sequence of events.

The main energy line activation will precipitate the enormous changes that will occur during the year of 1996. These changes will begin with the earth-masses being disturbed. This disturbance will activate the energy of the oceans to distort and violently respond. After the earth-mass activation then will come the responses from the volcanic structures. We cannot be responsible if you do not respond with the full force of spiritual activation. It is only through the activation of spiritual forces that you will survive. The energies that will be rampant upon the planet are not all negative. There are ones that are there to activate the spiritual energies. If you are involved with the material Third dimension, then you will be drastically affected when these changes begin.

We cannot emphasise enough the need to let go, surrender and become immersed within the spiritual forces. If you do not, you will be affected not only by the changes, but by the energies that belong to the spiritual field. These energies will cause many to abandon their structure and form within the dimensions of causality. They will be so affected that their bodies will disintegrate. By this we mean that none of the organs will function correctly. This energy will not affect those of you who have surrendered to the spiritual mantle once again. By surrendering your own wills to the will of the masters you will be surrendering back to the original plan.

The original plan was forecast many times during the life of the planet Earth in her Third dimensional state. She will again tell you of her plans, but this time in the form of cataclysmic disasters. By the end of the year 1995 the warnings will be obvious. Her cleansing operation will begin before this time and the outcome will already be present within the physical dimensions of the Earth.

After the activation of the first main line there will be activation from other lines. The first line governs the areas of Scotland, Nova Scotia, Mesopotamia and Sweden and Norway. This line will begin the cleansing. After that the minor lines affecting Spain and Italy, the islands of Majorca, Greece and Corsica will begin to cleanse also. Through the cleansing, the oceans will become filled with debris. There will be a time when this water will cause many problems. It is not possible to cleanse at this point in time; we must warn you not to attempt to carry out any schemes or plans to do so. The waters will be cleansed at a later stage, but not by chemical means. Many areas will be affected following the activation of energy clearance. We can only trust that you will not let go of your trust and strength when these possibilities become reality. It is only through thorough cleansing that the New Age will herald the beginnings of the New Order.

The second line of activation will be commenced shortly afterwards. This line begins in Portugal and stretches out to the extremes of the states of the USSR. Within its field are the countries of Switzerland, Bulgaria, Tasmania.

Qu: Are these lines complete circles, curves or just random design?
The lines themselves will occur where the energy field was completed. This actually requires you to surrender any preconceived ideas that there is any set design in the way of symmetrical shape.

Qu: Can you give me any more information in order to get rid of my own preconceived ideas?
Yes, we will attempt to show you how the lines are set out. Begin to think in terms of dials. These dials are like mandalas; they are positioned around the globe. The first dial was placed around the area now known to you as Spain, therefore the energy will be very strong

at the centre of this dial. The second dial was placed in the area of
Sweden. These dials span out to cover many miles of space and are
concentrated swirls of energy lines.

Qu: Does each dial have the same pattern of energy?
Yes, in the main, but these lines have become adulterated; therefore
the energy will give a different shape in each dial. When we have
cleared the energy fields, then the dials will retain their own design
very clearly. It is because of the adulteration that we must cleanse.
You are beginning to understand?

Qu: Yes. How have these lines become adulterated?
They have become adulterated because of the monstrosities that have
been performed with nuclear energy. This nuclear energy adulterates
the patterns. The explosions do not need to be in the immediate
vicinity to alter the patterns. The energy of nuclear is random. It does
not follow universal law.

*Qu: Am I understanding correctly here – that the dials should overlap each
other in certain areas creating a multi-dimensional span of energy lines?*
Yes, the pattern corrected would remind you of a diamond shape
overlaid many times with the same design as in an optical illusion. It
is a grid, but not as you would see a grid. This grid magnetises the
design to carry on repeating itself over and over, thus appearing as an
optical illusion. It would be too difficult for you to attempt to correct
your understanding in an analytical way. You must trust our com-
mands, so that the information does not become adulterated.

Qu: Is Tasmania correct as being connected to the second line activation?
Yes, it is correct. This part of the country is interconnected to the
states of Russia by interconnecting lines of energy forces. The energy
lines are brushing together within a vortex of energy.

*Qu: Can you explain this further to give me a picture of why it is therefore on
the second line activation?*
We will attempt to explain to you further the workings of the energy
system. Around the planet Earth are vortices of energy. These energy
vortices do not follow a symmetrical shape. They are twisting and
turning around their own centre. When one of these vortices con-

caves its energy forces, then the spurs of lines of energy that emanate are wildly emanating from the original central force. The energy itself does not follow a pattern. It will attempt to follow the lines of the spurs, but as these have become very adulterated, there is much confusion within these vortices.

Do not attempt to begin to understand the workings of the system of energy. You will only be confusing your minds into retrograde thinking. We will give you the continents and the countries of expected changes. Around the area known to you as Russia are many vortices of energy. You will see that this particular part of your world has many secret weapons. These weapons are nearly all working against the flow of universal energy. Before too long, this information will be given out from the central press agencies. Because of the activation of the laws of corrupt energy systems Russia herself will be indebted to the banks of repayment for a very long time. She will not recover herself after the transition. She will begin to usurp many of the corrupt politicians and their followers. It will be many many years before you will see the country of Russia regain any sort of power. Before the transition, Russia will engage in many events connected with power exchange. It will not assist her in the long term. Any actions now will need to be repaid.

Qu: How will the activation of the second energy line affect Portugal, Russia, Switzerland and Bulgaria?
These countries will be affected by whatever means it takes to cleanse the energy line. By this we mean that, after activation, any toxic waste within that particular line of energy will be dispersed. It will depend upon the type of toxicity that has affected the energy line. Some parts of the line are indeed very toxic. This is because of the energy of nuclear waste and also nuclear activation. The energy from the nuclear sources has adulterated the energy so much that the energy lines are bent and twisted.

We use analogies here, because as you know, you cannot see the energy; you can only feel it. At these points of twists and bends the energy does not flow, but builds what we would call cesspools. These cesspools of energy will not disperse without being activated from a higher energy vibration. They are very, very toxic. After activation

the cesspools will move; within this movement there will be much
energy released. When energy releases it causes many different
effects, much as if you were causing a fire bomb to explode. You
would receive the noise effects, the heat and also the aftereffects of
different air pollution and debris.

Qu: What sort of effects should we expect?
The effects that are most likely are to do with the weather. All
weather is controlled by energy; when the energy is negative then the
effects of the weather are also negative. We would anticipate that
there will be very strong winds, storms and electrifying lightning
flashes. The lightning flashes will disperse the energy around the
lines, but of course you will be in receipt of the fallout of energy
particles. Much has been said before of the effects of the storms which
are to befall your planet. These storms will disperse energy releases.
They will disperse particles of energy. A form of protection is to
retreat inside your own being; you cannot be affected by energy if
you have a solid protection. It will be as if you have on a radioactive
protection suit, one that will not let in rays of a certain vibration.

Qu: What other effects will ensue from the activation apart from the weather?
What other effects would you like? We are talking here of massive
energy releases; therefore massive energy being released through the
system of weather. Do not let your imagination run away from you.
This part of the synopsis is only to do with the cleansing. We have
not as yet approached the question of earth changes and movement.
Do not anticipate the worst – you would be wise to expect clearance
only.

Qu: Should I have had England in this second line of activation?
No, she has no clearance as yet to deal with. Her energy lines will be
cleared around the time of the equinox, when energy breaks through
the barriers within the time warp.

Qu: Do you mean this equinox this summer?
No, this will come when the time barriers are broken through, which
will be in the year 1996. You do not have to concern yourself with
England. She has many vortices of energy which protect her. She will

of course be connected with energy clearance, but in a much more minor way. Her energies have been purified many times before. It is much more apt for you to concern yourself with the approaching equinoxes, because of the energy that will be upon your planet. When you approach the time of the equinox it is much more important for you to celebrate this time, inviting in the energies of the devic kingdoms. It is then that the energies are more 'alive and kicking', as it were. You can utilise these energies; they are present for you to connect with. Do not deny yourselves the joy and happiness of celebration.

Chapter 10.

We must now begin to issue to you the answers of the many questions that worry you about the oncoming years. The most important ideas that will be presented to you are those of personal evolvement. Where you are, and what is actually happening within the Third dimension will not affect your personal development. You must now be willing to surrender any attachment to these planes of thought. It is only through complete and utter surrender that you will be able to complete the missions that were chosen so many years ago. We will be assisting you to progress to a point within your own evolvement, whereby the answers to the questions will not even be required.

It does not matter where you are or what you are doing, only that you are completely in tune with the master plan. We will be offering you much assistance with whatever you are doing when you are in tune with us. We cannot offer you more help than this. This means that when you are in the right place at the right time, then everything will be accomplished correctly, and everything will be accomplished on time. Timing will be of paramount importance.

It is important that the answers to your questions do not worry you. We are attempting to alter your states of awareness so that the questions do not even arise. There is no time to spend on speculation. You must all spend your time concerning yourselves with the objectives that you have set yourselves. These are separate from everything else. It is of no use trying to discover futuristic summaries of speculative thought. When we are in tune with you we will give to you any futuristic information that you require. Do not spend time idly prospecting details which in the main will not come about. Much time is being spent discussing ideas and formulations of what will and will not come about.

We will expect you all to come into the now, perform in the now, rejoice in the now and also to be content in this moment. Much of the energy that is being used on the planet is wasteful. It is not useful to anyone to speculate. Why speculate when anyone of you can receive direct useful answers to your questions? Do not attempt to set up discussion groups. They are of no use; they will only send you on wild goose chases around the globe, searching for safe places that do not exist, and answers to questions that should never have needed to be asked.

We cannot speak clearly enough on this subject. You must begin to understand that whatever happens is correct and that you will not need to understand all of the whys and wherefores. Do not attempt to be present when any of these discussions take place; they will reduce the energy count enormously. Intellectual discussion is no longer possible on any of the events that are looming up on your planet. Intellectual discussion will not be adverse to ego and personality interference.

Each one of you will be given all of the answers that you require in order to carry out the important work that you have to do. We have spoken before of individual tasks. These individual tasks must be carried out in a pure and correct manner. The only one that knows the correctness of the pathway is the one that has the task to carry out. We have spoken in haste because of the many people that are still gathering together to try to acclaim how and when things should be carried out. Your 'dials' of your own computers will give you the correct, exact details of the mission that you have chosen. Do not ask anyone else what they believe or even consider is correct. How could any of you completely ensure that the information you give another is correct when you have not, in some cases, unravelled your own linkage of data?

We will give you some direct information now on how one can unravel the coils of data included in your own information banks. The answer is to decode one by one any linkages that are given to you. Each one of you will be given small snippets of information when you are going about your lives. Do not hesitate to question why this and that is occurring. The way to question is to ask your higher self. By addressing your own higher self you are activating the pathways into the symmetry of the information banks. You will not receive answers if you do not attempt to ask for them. Even with your computer systems the answers will not be given until the question is directly given to the data banks.

You can begin to see yourselves as complex computer networks. Each different computer has completely different data banks. Therefore the only way of retrieving your personal information is to ask your data bank. There are no two people who have access to the same data banks. We are at present operating with a few data banks completely open, but many others completely sealed. It is as if the information is being given, but not accessed. Please do try now to realise that you are all separate in design, not separate from source. We are attempting to show you that you are all powered from the same source, but the information you will be receiving is vastly different.

When your electricity is received within your houses, much of it is used for light and heat, but some is also used for such delicate operations as ironing clothes. More is used for cooking and even producing scripts on electric typewriters. How could you expect an iron to instruct a typewriter to type? It is impossible! Remember now that one person who is instructed to say certain things is not always validated to instruct others in what they need to say.

There will be many instructors, many teachers, many healers, each one working with very individual energies, each one teaching what they have included in their data banks. There is only one common denominator, and that is personal choice and personal freedom, which must be common to all. Do not attempt to present your knowledge to anyone, expecting them to follow to the book what you are attempting to give them. The information is given to operate as a wake-up call, not categorised information, retained only by the intellectual areas of the mind.

Each word that is spoken is vibrated on a unique frequency when it is spoken from the heart centre. It is the frequency and vibration that is the important function of these words. Do you remember when your heart was open and the information that came from your lips did not appear to be you? Well, it was you the real you – you must now attempt to readjust the spoken word so that the only times you speak are the times that your heart requires you to do so.

Do not attempt to hold great rallies and question-and-answer sessions. These sessions only serve themselves and the egos of those presenting them. The only sessions we would suggest that you hold are those of silent retreat, during which time the energies of all those present will blend and harmonise without the presence of words and hypes. There has been far too much hype, even upon the more spiritual planes of thought.

Much can be accomplished with the silence of one's own vibration. We will attempt to be close to you during these times. If you are alone it is far easier for us to contact you. When more than one gather together in the name of Lord Sananda or Jesus Christ, then you will receive the gift of grace and much can be accomplished. But when you gather together in the name of intellectual discussion, or even some of your workshops which are not workshops at all, but market places for the sale of personal ideas, then the idea of grace would not even be touched upon. The energy rises to crescendos of excellence of compilation, excellence of speakers and excellence of receipt of money exchange. For what reason would this be useful? Only that it serves the Third dimensional frequency. You must now adjust everything within the framework of your lives which does not come from the highest of frequencies. The highest frequencies are given to you in your humble state not within the areas of personality acclaim and ego control.

These words may appear harsh, even insane. As we look upon your planes of existence, we are able to see that much more needs to be accomplished in the manner in which even the star-seeded ones are conducting themselves. Much is being lost because of ego control and self-satisfaction. We cannot assist you when you are continually controlling your own lives and attitudes. Do not attempt to readjust any of this information within your minds. Facts are facts and facsimiles are facsimiles. The new games that are being played are far more dangerous than the old ones. These new games can affect many more people; people are now in fear and disorientation. You must now adjust so that every aspect of your 'game' becomes the 'game' of the masters. If you consider the nature of the word 'master'. It has no weaknesses. It cannot be changed or adulterated, a master is a master, and ever more shall be so.

Do not acclaim yourselves as masters when you are still very much students. Students can group together in order to call down the energy and power of the Masters to teach you. You cannot teach each other, only support each other within the scope of your own ability. See yourselves now as supportive structures for the good of humanity, not the saving grace of humanity. It will be too late to adjust when you have reached the brink of calamity. This calamity will only be brought about by the egos and personalities that adulterate our information for personal gain and complacency of action. To be complete you must now attempt to gain your full spiritual mantles. These will be given as you give to us more and more of your trust and confidence. We will be present for another six months before the energies become too high for some of the people to adjust to the new frequencies. This time will come. We have warned of this, but to no avail. Many still sleep.

We will begin with the activation of the third line of energy. This line begins in Russia and ends in Tasmania. We will be confusing the issue if we begin to explain to you how and why this line is connected. The energy around the planet Earth does not, as we have previously attempted to explain, follow a fixed sequence. The energy lines are somewhat random compared to the ideas that many of you have in your minds as to energy cycles. The depth and breadth of each one of these 'lines' compares to nothing that you will have experienced before. It is not unlike the area known to you as a hologram. Within a hologram are many areas which coincide with the areas of energy within a 'line'. The function of these lines is to control the outflow and input of energy on your planet today. Because of the interference within each one of these lines, the energy is outpouring more than it is inflowing. By allowing you to see that the lines are not lines as such we can then expect that your capacity to understand will be far greater.

If we do not have some semblance of understanding then the information given will seem like pink elephants – unbelievable. We do not wish you to become so distant to the information that you are just becoming a robot. We do require that some of the information reaches the areas of your minds that can 'understand'. If we attempt to condense the information into too smaller particles, then the information will become devoid of essence and then of course useless. We will attempt to transform the way in which you perceive your universe into a much bigger, clearer and more precise picture.

After the activation of this third line of clearance, then the commotion on the planet Earth will convince many more people that there is in fact something going on that is not of the making of the people themselves. It will be a shock to the system of many when they realise that you have never been alone in this Universe and that there are many other beings present.

Before too long the need for intellectual confirmation will become obsolete. It is not too difficult to realise that many of the procedures that will take place can have no intellectual understanding. Without intellect you will find that many function much better. It is because of the rigidity of intellect that many have become very much of lesser intelligence. Without the function of intellect then the creative mind will come into play. When this begins then the anointing of the Holy Order will also begin. The anointing will take place as a ceremony within the heavenly bodies that are at present looking down upon your planet. We will anoint all of those who again take up their spiritual mantles. Because of the lack of understanding of those who choose to stay attached to the baser levels of existence, then we will also be pushed to pursue much cleansing of the morals and examples of conduct that are being performed upon your earth plane. Do not be concerned with the effects that such cleansing will have within your world. You will have chosen your own pathways which do not coincide with the more decadent alleys. These alleys are the scourge of mankind. They will be thoroughly cleansed.

Before the activation of the fourth and fifth lines of energy, the world will have become very much more subdued in temperament.

When one calamity after another has been given to the Earth to cope with then the minds of man will be somewhat dazed. When the world has reached this state the next activations will be carried out. We will be adjusting each strand of energy that has become in any way adulterated. Many energy lines have been tampered with. Each line will be checked with a fine 'tuning fork'. This will enable us to check for any lesions, frayed ends and malfunctioning systems. Each system or dial must function independently and in the correct manner. When we have adjusted the dials we will attempt then to correct the overall balance of the system.

After this exercise has been completed we will begin the structuring of the old masses into new ones. This does entail land movement.

Qu: Do we need to know which areas will be affected on these fourth and fifth lines?

It is of no consequence. By this time you will be firmly fixed within your own blueprints, it does not matter what happens within the Third dimension. It will not be fine details that you require, but an overall view of what is going on and why.

Qu: Does this complete the spring cleaning of the planet?

Yes, the minor details of cleansing will not be given. We must now begin to approach the task of explaining to you why the earth masses will move.

PART TWO

Chapter 11.

Massive shifts in the Earth's crust that will enable much of the energy caught beneath the surface to release

When the energy system of the Earth planet has been completed, she will feel somewhat top-heavy, or as you might feel, hung-over. This will happen because of the blueprint not fitting with the physical earthly structure. Therefore the blueprint of the physical entity will lock into a wobble or tremor. She will be attempting to align again with the blueprint within the etheric field of energy system. This system will be functioning directly in line with the cosmic energy system.

At this point the Earth will adjust her gait. She will become very much more in line with the structure of universal energy. At this point the energy from the source of her innermost quarters will begin to rise and fall. When this occurs, the energies from the inner crust will begin to surface.

Much of the structure of the Earth is contained within magma and lava-type substances. All liquids are movable and also drainable. By this we mean that some of this molten lava will flow out from the inner crust and begin to accrue much closer to the surface areas. Because of this movement the plates between the continents will begin to rise and fall. When this occurs the earth masses will also move. We anticipate that much of the area known to you as Yugoslavia will be moved further towards the area known to you as Russia. This will come about because of the extreme energy build-up between the plates under the ocean. Around the coastline of Yugoslavia are various layers of different levels of rock and cliffs. Because of this layering effect the ocean will be bounced up and down greatly when the cataclysmic action comes about. When the ocean moves in this way great surges of energy are released: the energy will bring about the movement of the plates. We would warn that much of the coastal areas of both Yugoslavia and Italy will be thrown into the ocean. During the ensuing crisis much of the military action will be curbed.

Qu: Which military action do you mean?
The military action which will be ongoing along the coastal waterways in this area. The military assembly has much to do during these times of crisis. We will warn you of these things, but not at the moment. It is very important that we begin to outline in more detail the synopsis of events that will befall your planet.

Colombia will fall greatly under the influence of earth changes. This continental mass cannot obscure the need for change. We cannot tell you when these events will take place exactly because of the energy activation. During the time of energy transference the mass of people will not respond, but during the time of energy line activation we are expecting that many more will again turn to the Masters. During this period it is possible to subdue energy transference. By this we mean that the energy escaping from the system can be subdued by the people. When you begin to align towards the heavenly hosts then energy is not lost, but is channelled backwards and forwards in a straight line from heaven to Earth. This will act as a buffer.

Because of these unknown quantities, we cannot anticipate how long it will be before the energy accumulates. What we can assure you is that there will be earth changes. The shape of the continents must be trimmed. This will enable a more select shape to be fashioned. When the Earth began her existence she did not appear as she does today. The earth masses were aligned; the shape was very formal. It does not occur to you that when a shape is irregular the energies are also irregular. Before too long you will be able to experience first hand what it is like to be regularly aligned.

Some time ago we had the information from one of your colleagues as to the upsurge of militancy amongst the light-workers. We are at liberty to address this problem. When the energies are released, the light-workers who are not truly aligned will suffer greatly. To be used as a line of light is truly humble, but it is not also worthy of you to sacrifice yourselves in this way. We ask that you allow us to use you as channels, but we do not require your sacrifice.

If you are to survive the times ahead, then you must now retrieve yourselves from the balance of power. By doing this you will guarantee your own survival and that of the planet. Can you see, dear ones, that we do not require you to become martyrs? We ask that you take now your opportunity to reclaim your rights, your power and your peace of mind. Before too long it will be too late to shout – 'wait for us'.

We can only give you the advice. Do you truly understand what is happening or are you just playing the game of survival? When one survives, one takes one's body along too. We can see that many of your bodies will not survive. It is as if you are using yourselves like lights on a Christmas tree so that people will gasp and say: 'Aren't they lovely!' If you are to be used completely as channels of light, then we require that you act as individuals. We can use these Christmas tree lights and will do so, as it is for the sake of the whole of humanity that we are placing all of our time and effort into this divine plan. But it will be a shame when some of these lights blinker and fade. What we are attempting to show you is that you must surrender. Surrender does not mean playing the game of light. This is no game; there are no rules, just surrender.

When you first descended onto this earth plane, you were aware of the plan. Now that it has been so long between 'acts' you begin to wander. Do not wait for the end. It is not the end, but the beginning – the beginning of something wonderful. Can you see that we are attempting to wake you from the sleep, you are still dreaming? Come now into full awareness; there are no martyrs required. Some of you are definitely attempting to look 'holier than thou'. We do not require any particular dress code; just that you surrender now to your own soul pathway.

We will now return to the object of addressing earth movements during the time of change. This time of change will have many different aspects. The time of change will be coined by many, but alas understood by very few. When it is time to change then everything must align with the new. In this way we will be providing you with the 'layers' of change that are upon your planet Earth. She will be revolutionised.

Much has been activated now, in the minds of man, of the oncoming changes. We cannot give you exact amounts of time that will indicate when and where the great earth-mass changes will occur, but we can indicate the extreme areas of change. We will be adjusting the information as we go along. Because of the extreme energy changes, there are no definite decisive actions that can be logged. The changes are all very much affected by the adverse action of the negative energy releases. It is because of this that much will be activated during this time in the form of a synopsis of events that will possibly begin. As the time approaches towards the millennium, every event will have been exposed; but for now we will give warnings. These warnings can be adjusted if we have constant contact with all of those who are able to converse with us. We must have your complete attention. We cannot give you exact timings. As the time approaches for any of the changes we will be present to give you more information. We cannot adjust, but we will certainly advise.

Around the Mediterranean there will be much wind change, which will cause many adverse happenings. These happenings will begin the tremendous earth mass changes that are destined for Greece and Scotland. Because of the nature of wind and velocity, the amount of time that this will take will be unknown, but we can assure you of the changes. Much of the land cultivated within the Scottish Highlands has been undergoing changes for some time. The locals are aware of this. The edges of the oceanic landways are crumbling; the mountains do not now seem as inviting. You have seen the disasters that have been occurring within the mountainous areas; these are not just fate.

The energy present within these mountain ranges has altered considerably. Because of the energy you are experiencing, many climbers have suddenly become afraid; they do not know why or even how. As time proceeds you will experience even more frightening events on these particular mountain ranges. As energy expands and becomes more active, the rays or waves of frequency are somewhat peculiar. This does not require any scientific explanation. It only requires that you regard this information as advice. Do not venture into these areas. They are now very much out of bounds for those who wish to survive. As time passes you will also begin to realise how much easier it is to begin to understand each and every event that occurs upon the planet Earth.

We will begin to give you much more understanding, and therefore warning, of the entire planetary energy system. It is not because of the energy that these happenings will occur, but because of the lack of energy vitality that is occurring within the planetary system. After the activation of energy lines you will begin to sense that everything will become purified. Each energy line activation will begin to wake up the senses that you already possess, but have never used. Misalignment of these energy lines has been somewhat of a dampener for all of the beings present on the earth plane. When the activations begin you will begin to realise that much has been misaligned and then the awakening of your own senses will also begin.

When energy is misaligned, anything and everything within this field of misalignment responds accordingly. It is not that you do not understand; it is that you do not respond when the energies are being filtered in the wrong way. We must attempt to begin to give you much more sensibility. When the energy has been realigned, then you will begin to understand how and when the changes will occur. What we must attempt to bring about is the opening of your sensing devices that have for many years lain dormant.

If we were to give you the understanding of these motions you would not then awaken your sensing devices. The mind always begins to control if it is allowed to do so. We do not require your minds to realign at this particular moment; we do require that your senses begin to awaken. Sensibility is something that has been allowed to become very much something of an unknown quantity. During the oncoming years you will never choose to see this again. There are many who have their senses aligned now to the oncoming events, but because of the nature of mankind they are not using this information. We will begin to send you great surges of energy which can awaken any who are not properly awakened. When these surges are experienced those receiving them will awaken instantaneously.

By the end of your summertime the events that are propelled into action will have begun the onslaught that will lead to the planet Earth completing her cleansing process. Do not be afraid, when as we have explained, many areas become almost uninhabitable. It is not because we wish to harm, but because we wish to cleanse that these events will come about. We will not be able to give you an immediate motion of such events. We will not be able to approach any of these disasters with absolute precision. For some time now the energy has been building around many of the areas which will be given a boost of cataclysmic action in order to release such negativity.

Do not be alarmed if what we say is going to take place does not take place at that precise time. These events will be given over to you as much for guidance as for precise timing. Our timing does not coincide with anything within your own mental capacities. Timing is a man made entity, it holds no credence within the universal continuum. By about October of this coming year the energies will be very much 'on top of you'. We will refer to the energies again and again until you are able to understand what is actually happening to your planet. Many other planets have undergone this same cataclysmic action. The energies that have been altered have always served the purpose to which they were aligned. We cannot expect you to understand what you have never had within your own 'mind's eye'.

Everything of which we speak is part of God's plan not our own. Our plans have no volition. Do not now begin to adulterate any of the words that are given to you here. They are words of truth. They will speak clearly and concisely to your innermost soul, not your mind. Our minds do not have their own personality, we have no duality; only the one mind.

Because of this action of personalities, many are still attempting to control their destinies. Control will only lead to disaster of a kind that will unleash many more disasters. Do not attempt to control; it is only through surrender that you can be assured of your own survival. Man has controlled and destroyed. Before too long you will witness many who are still attempting to struggle along the path of damnation, turn and ask, 'What is the truth?' Can you be there to tell them?

We will assist any of you who will choose to be present in the now and the unknown. Each and everyone of you can assist at this time, not from your minds, but from your souls, your souls that now hang upside down within the framework of society. It is as if you have had to turn upside down in order to perceive that there is a greater truth. One that does not hang well within the structure of the society that had control. Can you perceive how and when we will be present with you? Can you perceive what it will be like to walk hand-in-hand with the hierarchy?

We do not wish to lead you into temptation, but we will attempt to draw you closer and closer into our world and your newly awaiting bliss. As time goes on, closer and closer will be our contact. The contact you have acquired up to this point will be thought of as superficial after the turn of the century. We will be with you first-hand, not only in speech, but in touch and sensuality.

This is Master Hilarion who does not always appear as the Master, but appears to many of you as Chief Seattle. After much praise and abuse, Chief Seattle is now considered amongst you as a prophet. It has been an easier task for my image to be seen as Seattle rather than as Hilarion. I am responsible for the undertakings of the planet's ecology system. I have been amongst many of you, during medita-tion and during prayer. I am truly grateful for the opportunity to approach many more of your peoples through the guise of Seattle. It would not have been as easy to present some of the material that has been presented, if not for this gentleman's persona.

The medicine wheel of time has been given in order for the persona of Seattle to ingrain itself upon your minds. This wheel will bring about much activation and much praise.

Qu: Has this medicine wheel of time already been given to us?
No, this wheel will be presented during the oncoming year. It has to be reinvented during this century. The reinvention must come about in order for the information to be considered authentic. The old wheel of time does not serve you now.

Qu: Could you give us more information of the significance of this wheel and how it can be used?
Yes, the information encoded in the wheel will enable you to travel in

time, across and down depth and breadth. It is a type of time chariot. The chariot will direct you to the areas that are unknown – the areas that do not carry the mantle of thought patterns and understanding. The old wheel controls your minds, controls your thoughts. The new wheel will not be in any form of control. The mind responds to symbols. Without symbols there will be freedom of passage: passage to the space known as 'no time'. By December of the year 1996 much will have passed into the time scale of 'no time'.

Qu: Will there be a period when we are both in and out of time?
Yes, but this will not be a correct way of explaining this occurrence. The time known as 'no time' will be co-handled within the function of time.

Qu: What will this feel like?
It will occur to you suddenly, without explanation. You will not know that you are within the field of no-time, but will only realise that you have begun to activate again when you return to time. By March of your coming year, the end of the time continuum known to you as consecutive time will be upon you. It will be as if time has ended. The energies present at this time will make it impossible for you to judge time accurately. Do you not now feel that time is running out? Well, it is, but not as your intellectual minds understand it. You will be allowed to exist in time only until the end of 1995.

Qu: How will this medicine wheel of time be brought to our plane?
When the time is right, the energy of the medicine wheel will again reach your planet. It will be given to one who has the knowledge of the medicine wheels, one who does not at this moment require the information, but will nevertheless receive it. It will be through the energy of the other medicine wheels that this will be accessed.

We must end now with the note of compliance. This note will subject you to the onslaught of energies that will be received within the next two years on your Earth planet. Our note is the one of do-ray-me, it does not refer to the notes of the piano, but to the notes of the rays from the Sun that descend upon you.

Qu: What does this mean?

We have no way of showing you how much energy descends upon you from the Sun, but through chanting the energy tune of do-ray-me you will feel the energy from the Sun beating within your own bodies. If you are aligned to these energies, then you will receive the new energies that descend from the heavens with dignity.

We will begin today with the information that will enable you all to be present at the beginning of 'time'. At the beginning of 'time' the energy that was upon your Earth plane was completely different to the energy that is now present.

For your information we will begin to describe to you how it was. The Earth plane was not bound in time. The energy was completely free and boundless. By this we mean without destination, without rules or boundaries. These boundaries that have become your prison walls will need to be removed, so that the energy of the universal system can prevail.

After mankind was placed upon this Earth plane, he became somewhat adventurous. The adventures that he began to place himself within were not becoming. They were not real adventures in the true sense, but enabled mankind to become entrapped. The problem is that you do not realise what freedom you have until you lose it. Because of this mankind travelled a path of adventure, but loss of freedom. He was unaware of this; awareness did not come until later.

Because of the pathway that mankind has travelled, there is a need now for you to understand the whole journey – not just this later part of the journey where mankind is being forced to awaken fully. We have undertaken to guide you now through the mire on a path of fulfilment and total wakefulness.

This shift in awareness will be part of the structure of the oncoming years. We have much to teach you and much for you to learn within our sphere of awareness. Do not approach this information as revolutionary; it has always been with you, but not accessed. We are using our energy to access for you. You have all become very sleepy. Upon our plane the energy has the action of mobilisation – we cannot fall asleep; we do not wish to do so.

Our journey so far has taken us to many different energy levels; we will travel on further. After the continuum of universal energy levels has become stable, we will be with you teaching you more and more. You will become as one of us, but will only be able to teach those who have not yet reached your level of awareness. Many will be stranded upon the Earth plane after the first wave of ascension. These people will require you to rescue them. This rescuing will be carried out via many different levels of energy activation.

For some there will be much exercising of energy display. By this we mean that energy will become visible to some. In other ways you will show how far you have advanced. Those people who have already been activated a little will then grab the opportunity to further their awakening. By displaying your energy capabilities you will be allowing those of less activation to see what is possible.

Do not become afraid to be a part of this display. We cannot allow any of the souls who wish to grow to become like pebbles on one of your beaches. They are not deadened, they have a spark of light glowing within them and this must be allowed to ignite and burst into full flaming glory. During your night walks you may take a candle with the one flame, but if you were accompanied by many with their flames, then there would be a mass of light, so much so that one could hardly believe there was darkness.

The advancement of six souls will be required to upgrade the awareness in any group of twenty-five. By this we mean that an average upgrading will occur when the group of twenty-five have been led by the six who have already awakened. It will take the power of the six to raise the consciousness of the twenty-five. This cannot be broken down any further. There are many formulae that you do not have the capacity to understand as yet. We will feed you numbers and places, but cannot always back up these words with an understanding which will make any sense to you. As time goes by you will begin to understand, but not by logical means.

We see now that you are beginning to appreciate the wording of the 'time' phrases. Is it not incredible that for many years these phrases have been used, but never understood? In your time you have seen many adulterations of phrases and wording, but some of these old phrases still are used many times. 'Once upon a time' could never have been coined unless the adage of time had been invented. Time was never meant to be. Time was time which was unknown. Time is endless, incomprehensible and never to be split and divided. This was completely man-made not God-given. You were given an endless eternity. Dream your dream awake, for within the dreaming you will recapture any of the dreams that you have given away. Many dreams were edited, mutilated and therefore lost when man chose to activate only his wishes and desires.

Man alone could not have given himself the gifts that were bestowed upon him before 'time'. It is as if you have returned all of the gifts until you have the total realisation that you are worthy of them. Was this not the only lesson that requires to be learnt! Are you not all, still, affirming to yourselves that you deserve love and abundance? We are often time amused by the incongruity of the difficulties that you have tied yourselves up in. These gifts were yours. You did not need to return them, but one day you will rejoice in the reasoning.

The information on the earth-mass changes will be filtered through when you are least expecting this. We do not wish to shock any of you. Our methods are ones of kneading and softening the material of both our information and your minds before we deal the cards to you. When you are tuned to your souls the information will be received without shock or horror. Do we not weave a good cloth?

When you are happy and receptive it does not matter if the car does not operate or if the house burns to the ground. You just filter the information through your minds and then burst into action. We are kneading and softening your hardened attitudes. Love has a great part to play. Love as a universal energy fluid will soften and mould to a more receptive form. This form has room for growth. It does not snap when moved out of its usual shape. There is no usual shape – only flexible, loving, movable form. It loses nothing when the shape is changed. Think of your play material for children. It feels good to mould this material, change its shape and allow any creative feeling to express itself within this material. Think of yourselves as play-dough material where the creative spirit can shine through you in whatever form it chooses.

As you become mellow, you are sweetened by the spirit of love. Without this spirit of love everything begins to go sour; you will perceive any of this information as catastrophic without the feelings of love which we bring to you. How could we tell you that the physical world as you perceive it will break up into many pieces, if we did not bring this news with love? When you are softened, the information will just become something that you require, but have no comments about. You will have no answers and no questions; just complete acceptance of the period of your so called 'time' that is ahead of you. When your perception has sharpened to perceive time as it really is, then you will no longer even require the information. Being present in the holy moment will be adequate for you too.

We have had to come and release you from the trap you set yourselves when you invented 'time'. Because of the 'time' factors involved there has to be much movement within the areas of the mind. As 'time' goes on you will begin to experience the dimension of duality of mind even more, because of the oncoming energy releases. As the frequency of the new energies rise, then the old energies become more obvious. Before the overthrow of any government there is always a battle of wits and power. It is the same scenario that will be played over and over again until you allow the new frequency to control your mind. Do not fight too long. The war will be over before you can decide which side you wish to be present on.

As much energy escapes between the dimensions there will be several occasions when energy will overpower you, and then you will have no decision to make. This will begin the 'time warp' period, when 'time' neither stands still nor moves.

My friends, do not tarry on this path, be quick of foot and deft of mind. It is then that the path becomes easy, quick and eventful. Obvious decisions will come your way, not decisions of which you are used to, but decisions that will lead you onwards and outwards towards the continuum of universal energy resources. It is a bounteous place, this Universe; it does not compare with anything within your comprehension.

After the oncoming energy releases you will see many who cannot keep the pace. These people will then become somewhat atrophied.

We speak now of those who have not begun the awakening process. These individuals will not be going home, but will journey on towards another sphere where their energies can be exploited in the way of the warrior around the wheel of rebirth and then, again, will come the opportunity for self-realisation.

Chapter 12.

We will be approaching now the information that will assist you with the oncoming earth-mass changes. These changes will be appropriately addressed in the order of the need of your peoples' attitudes. When we are giving you this information we will be required to address certain issues which will not sit easily with you. These issues must be addressed. We cannot and will not temper the information in order for your minds to remain closed.

By the end of this coming year the energy will be evident to you in many different ways. Before too long you will be able to adjust your own energy fields to compensate for the changes. We will be explaining to you how the Earth herself will adjust in order to compensate for the changes. These changes will involve many different areas becoming somewhat readjusted. These readjustments will be in the form of earth shifts. The earth shifts themselves will allow the energy residing beneath the surface to be released. As usual the energy will not be present for very long, but will undoubtedly cause many upsets whilst it is present.

Before too long the energy that has released will form great energy balloons which must be released into the main universal energy stream. As energy releases it accumulates many different vibrations. These vibrations are not ones that you would associate with. They are vibrations that contain different elements of energy. Energy has been considered very much as a specialised entity, but none are investigating the numerous forms of energy. By the turn of the century your scientists will have undoubtedly begun to understand the vastness of this field of discovery. This will not come about by investigation in a scientific manner, but through seeing and believing. The vastness of this area of life has up until this point in 'time' been quite unseen, unspoken, and not at all revered.

Whilst we remain anonymous to the energy regime we gain our position of power through our anonymity. They are at present contriving to make contact with many different types of beings, but do not allow themselves to be in contact with us. It has been known for some time that your governments are allowing certain individuals to come in contact with certain of the extra-terrestrial beings. These beings do exist within a certain code of energy control. We do not. Other beings have been present within the sphere of your Earth plane for many generations. They have come to assist the passage of the Earth planet. We accept that, for the present time, it would be impossible for your governments to even comprehend that they are not in control and will never be in control. We will be contacting them ourselves within the next two years. By that time it will be necessary for some of the eyes to be opened. We cannot open all eyes at once. This would cause the backlash of energy that accompanies fear.

One by one we will open the eyes of all of those individuals who ask from their hearts to have more knowledge of the Universe and the planets around you. By December of this coming year the energy will be so strong that no one will be able to disguise their awareness. As the energy becomes full strength, many will attach themselves to certain units or structures of community lifestyle. We will be approaching many of these units. Some will be able to cope with the strength of the energy, but others will not. It is because of the strength of spiritual awareness that some of these communities will be in full health and expansion at this time. Others will not be forming through a spiritual network, but through a fear aspect of themselves. We will not attempt to interfere, as many will need the group energy to adjust to the oncoming changes.

Fear will be the worst enemy at this time, for through fear you will be activating many of the energy lines that are held within the Earth and within the ocean beds. As you begin to activate fear, then you will also activate any of the negative energy within the physical being of the planet. We are activating many of the energy lines that belong to the atmosphere and stratosphere. You will be activating the lines that lie deep within the Earth. These lines do need to be cleansed, but this would occur naturally after the main energy line activation. Through fear the energy lines within the planet Earth will react and physically release. Much of this releasing will cause energy build-ups. These build-ups will then operate more cataclysmic action.

Can you see that if we can convince you of the love and compassion that you will be receiving at this time, then you will be safer and move swiftly through the changes into the next millennium of 'time'? Fear will kill quicker than any disaster that we could forewarn you of. Fear is the enemy. Love will keep you strong and healthy, you will be forewarned of the changes, you do not need to group together in fear. As you travel the path of love and acceptance you will experience much fun and abundance. We do not jest; it is still possible to adjust to these energies and be at ease within your own bodies and minds.

Do not be afraid of these energies. They are there to enable you to fulfil your destinies – not take away your destinies. Do you begin to understand what it is that we are saying? Right action is taking place on your planet and will continue to do so. We do not attempt to apprehend you; only adjust now everything in order for the occupation of the planet to become a holy one. Holy Order will be given to you from the time that the planet has ascended to her rightful position within the energy field of the Universe.

After the summer months have passed there will be some semblance of order within the devic kingdom. The devic kingdom has been neglected, but there are many now who are in contact with these devas. Much neglect has accumulated energies within the devic kingdom that also must be cleansed. We have adjusted many of these energies before, but they have always become 'dirtied' again. This time we will insist that energies from chemicals are not returned to this kingdom. The energies that are used within your agricultural fields are destroying many of the finer energies within the devic kingdom. This must not be so, we will adjust any of these energies as they are used. You will find that their power will be adulterated, therefore the growth necessary will not occur as expected. This action must be practised until all of the 'dirtier' energies have been cleansed then it will become impossible to alter the fields again.

Once these energy sequences have re-established themselves, then the plant kingdom will become perfect. It has its own perfection field. This perfection will not allow you to infiltrate. Have you not been aware of the changes within nature? There are many plants that have become extinct. They will not grow within the areas that are neglected on an energy level. The system within which plants grow is very sensitive. It is more sensitive than the energy system within which man has grown. The energy levels must be at least that of subsistence, for plant life to even exist. It is the energies that are obsolete, not necessarily the goodness in the soil.

You will have experienced sometimes that a plant will grow where there is no sign of goodness in the soil, but it will not grow where the energies have reached a certain level of neglect. You can grow anything anywhere if you give the plants enough respect and love. They thrive on love. Many of you have begun to become more in tune with nature. This must go even further. It is time to embrace the things of Nature, walk hand in hand with them. Journey with them, they are your friends, your allies on this path. It is the energy of Nature that will sustain you during these times of strife.

Nature will not be affected as much as yourselves; she will serve as a healing tool for all of you. Nature does not have an emotional energy field, only a spiritual one. Your energy field will be losing its emotional dependence, therefore you will be able to cohere with Nature much much more. She does not now respond to the fields of emotion from human beings, she only responds when she is approached from the feeling of love or spirituality, both being the same energy. We choose our words in order for you to understand both worlds. It is the emotional energy that has caused you to create the madness on this planet. Without emotion she will reign supreme. Take back your spiritual mantles and rejoice with the planet in all her supremacy.

For some time now you have been inquiring for the information on relationships, we are ready to give you some of the basic understandings that you will require for the next stage of your growth.

Relationships have a small part to play in the next stage of growth for humanity. Relationships are divisions of oneness; they are secular and unstable. The oneness regime is the one which we are inviting you into. This oneness does not require relating to. It is what it is. Unfortunately many of you are still hankering for the oneness with just one individual. We do not advise any of you to end your relationships, but to expand them now to include everyone. You will soon experience that oneness has many avenues. The avenues which have been closed to you before will be opened. Oneness has no divisions, it has no boundaries.

We will be feeding you much more information on oneness as the energies heighten. You will be able to understand more as your energy fields expand to allow much more relating on many different levels. It is then that you will begin to understand the limitations of your so called sexual unions. One man -one woman, would be all that was required for many of you to begin to understand union, but you are not in unions, you are involved in dependency and repression. We must congratulate many of you for leaving these so-called relationships in order to further your paths.

For some time now the energies within the sexual fields of your beings has become very fibrous. By this we mean that the energy has become filamented, it is in many strands; the union of sexuality has become adulterated. The act itself does not give you harmony, but only comfort. For many years the planet has itself been infertile. Her body is well used, over used, abused. She does not feel good about herself. It is similar with your own bodies, you have abused them and misused them. Do not be surprised at the levels of disease and distress that this has caused. If you had real sexual union you would not be experiencing these kinds of illnesses.

Do not now begin to adulterate our words. It is not sexuality that is wrong, but the attitude of the people to sexuality. If we had the essence of sexuality in a couple of people, then we would be able to bottle this essence and feed it to the rest of the people. But we do not; the essence has long gone. It is the residue of decadent sexuality that is present within your people. There are many that are removing themselves from the sexual playground. They are aware at this moment that the sexuality of which we speak does not give them happiness but only despair.

During the oncoming years, when the energies have balanced once again, then you will begin to see that the pure union of spiritual beings will again produce the pure essence of sexuality. This essence is as pure as the driven snow; it holds no guilt, no fear and no adulteration. The pure essence of sexuality holds the secrets of ecstasy for you. It is in the blissed-out state of pure spirituality that the union of pure sexuality is produced.

We will be giving you now the earth-mass movements in detail. These earth changes will coincide with the energy movements within the perimeters of the Earth's crust. The earth-mass movements will bring much loss of life and also much chaos. This is inevitable; it cannot be altered. Because of this information we have attempted first to soften your hearts, open your hearts and allow you to interpret the details of this information from your hearts.

Much of the land within the southern hemisphere will become energised. It is through this energising that the landmasses themselves will begin to move. Around the coast of Australia much of the land will subside and fall into the ocean. We cannot alter this; it is not so much to do with the energy of the people as the energy of the landmass.

New Zealand has many inlets of energy that will be released. After the releasing, the landmass will bulge and concertina into a more concentrated form. After this the energy of New Zealand will become very high. It is one of the safest areas on the planet as far as energy is concerned. This energising of New Zealand will bring about much movement of people. People will want to be in the vicinity of this energy. It will attract many groups of people searching for areas to settle and make a home. We do not anticipate that the population will expand greatly, but there will be much sorting of who should, and who should not be present on this particular land-mass. It has the ability to shake and vibrate for long periods, but still remain stable. The energy has been increasing in this area since the beginning of 'time', and will not now be demolished. The concertina-ing effect will not cause as much damage as might be expected. It will not damage much of the land. As energy doubles and blows out it causes the land to adjust but will not necessarily cause devastation from a worldly viewpoint. This concertina-ing will gradually form a duct of energy which will serve as a spout or lip for relaying energy to other areas in your world.

Much of Australia has accumulated negative energy, but again she will not be devastated, only adjusted according to the flow of new energy that she receives. Australians in general will adapt. It is only during such crisis that the true spirit of the people will become obvious. At this moment in time the Australians have much pleasure and fun, and not really a lot of spiritual awareness. During the oncoming crisis times, the people will readjust their spiritual mantles, and wake up in order to cope with the land mass injuries. It will only be injuries that she sustains; not complete obliteration. Much of the energy held in this particular area has been released through the fire, but there is more to come. This time it will be released through the energy of water and air. Much flooding, more winds than have ever been experienced and indeed 'torrential' rainfall. For the people there will be times when they believe that nothing will heal. The sight of such rainfall and water-logged areas is not something that they are expecting, but it will subside and clear. As the water clears, much of the coastline will be lost to the sea and indeed fall away.

Within the areas known to you as the South Pacific, many islands will cease to be; others will rise and become more of a consolidated landmass. This will cause the islanders to congregate within the larger mass of land, therefore building a community that has never been so close. Before the energy subsides, many will capture in their own imaginations what is going on, and also what they must do. They are very intuitive people and will again revert back to the pureness of their natures.

We will be attempting to give you much more warning as the time becomes closer to these events occurring. It will not be so that you can run away, but so that your consciousness can encapsulate the information and ease away any fear and discomfort from the events taking place on the planet. If you are warned, then you are able to accept without cause for concern.

Can you see now how our plan works? We will provide you with all of the information that you require. By allowing you to assimilate now, we will be making the pathway clearer for you in the future. If you are aware of futuristic events then you do not feel out of control, and as if there are demonic forces unleashed upon the planet. These forces are definitely not demonic. They are themselves clearing the demonic energies that have been produced by man, over centuries of controversy, battles and self-interest. If we did not come now, you would be destroyed.

We cannot watch any longer as you continually rape and pillage the planet's resources without any remorse or guilt. Even now your ecology groups have very much their own self-interest at heart. They do not concern themselves with the heartfelt feelings that should be felt for the planet herself. Have you heard any ecologist talk of the energy that has been built up over the centuries as man has been self-centred and self-imposing? We will not try to make them understand. We will instead clean these energies. One by one you will experience our energy activation impulses. These impulses will not be lightly given, they will be given with the power of the Almighty.

The hand of God will serve mankind with the blow to awaken him from this deathly sleep. We have waited many years to be able to serve the hand of God. We do not concern ourselves with the energy releasing but only perform our duty. Our hands are tied to the hand of God; we do not try to struggle away. We are content and at home within the vicinity of the highest energies present within the universal system. You too will be able to experience these energies as you choose to return home.

We will return now to give you more details of changes within the earth-masses. Energy will be releasing from the coastline of India into the Indian Ocean. We have already approached the coastline of Calcutta. This area is fast becoming explosive; she has not as yet released. We cannot always accurately foretell the 'timing' for you, but as always, endeavour to warn you beforehand. Many areas of the Indian Ocean will experience mammoth tidal waves. These waves will spill onto the coastal mainland, encroaching into the urban areas and freeing up many of the restricted land energy lines. These lines will need to be freed from the dark, dank negative energies that they have contained for many years. After some time the energy will again release – this time into the ocean, from the landmass. This will enable much of the damaged mainland to become stable again.

We are not always able to satisfy your intellectual needs for understanding, but always we are endeavouring to give you enough information to stimulate your own codings. All of you have these changes coded into your systems. You do not need all of the details. Information on the basic ideas will suffice to activate your own genetic codings which foretell of these changes. Much of the channelled information that is being imparted to your planet is only to activate your codings. It is basic material which stimulates and activates the codings. If this material is edited it will not activate the codings. Each word, each sentence is aligned in such a way that the essence is given but without frills, without diversity. When the truth is spoken it does not need to be understood, it only serves as a catalyst for your own truth mechanism.

These mechanisms within your own system must be activated. We cannot give you all the details. The truth lives within each one of you, not outside you. Much of what is said in your world is not real, it is only for the sake of speaking and hearing one's own voice that most people communicate. Do not communicate if you have nothing real to say. You must now be more precise with your own wording. We do not have time to converse with you on topics that are not important. The only important matter is the salvation of the planet Earth. She is your source of all life, you must not destroy her. We will not allow it to happen. Apart from the marauding conversations, we are at liberty to say that you are all too concerned still with your own state of wellbeing. This wellbeing does not come from the quarters of your spiritual being, but from the accumulation of wealth and rewards. We cannot speak enough of the need to surrender. You must surrender. Surrender your arms and your energies unto the Father.

We are awaiting the time when we will no longer need to give such long discourse on this particular subject. It is only because of the wills of men that we have need to continually approach the desires and demeanours of the people of your planet. She will escape the negative build-up of energies. You must ensure that you will also. We cannot give you complete programmes of events when the need for them is always tied in with your own safety. You are safe. You will not be obliterated. Allow your own blueprints to show you the way and the end. This end is not the end of the planet Earth. Hear our words and do not doubt us again. We cannot continually reassure you of the high spiritual nature of our actions. Be as one. This oneness will give you the confidence that you all require to carry on 'treading water' as the multitude of changes begin.

Around the area of southern America much will alter. There have been many predictions for the salvation of the area of Los Angeles. It is a salvation plan. Part of this island of land will remain, but will be pushed inward towards the deserts of Nevada and Arizona. Much of the land will be lost, but you will be able to make contact with the many islands of small encrusted earth matter that are at present sunk below the ocean. This will be made possible by the energy of the releases, causing great landmasses to move and reassemble. It will be as if there has been a removing of all debris, but not of the earth structure. Because of the movement of the plates, some land will remain, but not in the shape that has been assembled before. Too much of the land has corroded for the same areas to remain. Much corrosion of land energy has caused the corrosion within the physical manifestation.

We do not wish to cause concern where there is no need, but we must attempt here to allow you the freedom to interpret our wording within the framework of your own understanding. The areas that have not before been above water levels will now appear. It is not a dream, we speak of massive shifts in energy and therefore physical matter. Do not appraise these words, allow them to reach the consciousness of your mind. They will lie in the depths of your mind until the time that the energy is released. You will realise then the truth. We do not require you to understand, but just allow the essence of our words to enter through the membranes of the mind. The end result will be one of complete acceptance. Do not query; queries will lead you into misunderstandings.

After the activation of the main energy 'lines', some semblance of order will be maintained within the system of energy that surrounds the planet Earth. This semblance of order will be maintained, but will be the call for the Earth to realign her physical structure according to the energy surrounding her. She cannot be allowed to remain in the chaotic state when the energy patterns have become pure. You cannot be allowed to stay within her physical presence if your energy does not match that of her grid system. One by one the energies present will cleanse your own auric fields. If you cannot adjust, then you will not exist within the field of the planet Earth.

Chapter 13.

We will be assuring you of the passage which you take. Any passage taken with the wholeness of spirit will lead you to the ultimate destination of oneness. Our aspirations for you are two-fold: one that you survive, and two that you join with us in the areas of ultimate choice and wisdom. Do not be wary of what we are giving you as a goal. This goal is ultimately the one which you desire. It is as if you do not yet know who you are and what you are. We will be attempting to give you any of the information that you will require on your path of self-realisation.

Because of the energy releases, much of the area known to you as Russia will be forgotten. This energy release will cause much devastation, and loss of control for the governmental powers of Russia. In the past the land has been devastated from nuclear energy explosions. It cannot now be left in this state. We will cleanse, but because of the area that is concerned here, there will be much devastation. We cannot cleanse without doing a thorough job. The job at hand is vast, the energy will be thorough. Many of the areas connected to Russia will also be affected. We will be producing an effect that will shower many of the connecting areas with a cleansing energy. This will not be without due cause. These areas also are contaminated. The energy surrounding Russia is less contaminated, but nevertheless negative in nature.

The nature of energy in its pure state is one of pure light. This light when experienced by mankind will begin to decode more codings. We cannot suggest to you any way of warning these people, apart from the words that we offer. The words that we speak, speak to your souls. Within your souls are many facets of light energy. When these different facets of light energy are enlivened, then the being awakes. Because of the difference in soul energies, we cannot give you numbers and degrees of awakenings. It is purely a question of what and when the soul remembers. We will be activating many who did not dream they would be activated. It is as if some are rubbing their eyes now and wondering what has happened to them. They do not yet remember what it is they must do, but they have become awake. This awakening will stay with them. After some time the awakened ones will become enlightened. In order to become enlightened they will require the information that we are at present imparting to some people. This channelled information has a great part to play in the enlightening of souls that have awakened. In the half-awakened state they will not respond; it is when their eyes are opened.

During the second half of next year many will storm your churches, storm your governmental offices, in order to awaken the new order. It cannot be carried out in this way. The only way is through the activation of more souls. We cannot advise you on every event, but we will endeavour to guide if you ask us. We cannot be responsible for the laws of awakening. Each soul will interpret our information differently, but so be it. Each soul has a place on the spectrum of evolution.

When you are approached by a snowstorm, you do not all retreat inside. Some will gather wood, some will go and play, others will contemplate the next sunshine. We cannot make any of these decisions wrong; they are only different. Because of the nature of attitudes there will be many who see this time as a time of revolt. Revolt will not turn the heads of the decadent. Decadence reigns supreme during revolts. It will be another year or two before the energy runs smooth. When the energy is running smooth you will be experiencing much bliss and ecstasy.

Before too long the energy holding the British Isles will begin to erupt. During this eruption any energies that are not of the highest will be exposed. Much has already come to light, but there is more to come. Many of your politicians will resign, be it a cowardly act. They do not respond well under attack. But they will be under the attack of the higher energy fields. Former intellectuals will begin to ease into a new way of communicating. This way will be the way of the future. Your future depends upon the activating of the creative principle, both within your education system and your politics.

Do not create the bubble which will burst when energy becomes over energised. We warn you here of transformation too quick and in too intense a way. The opening of the creative mind is a delicate thing. It can be over-exposed too quickly and will then burn out. This burn-out causes much stress and over stimulation of the brain cortex. When you are teaching your children, allow them to stimulate themselves. They will do this if it is allowed. You do not need to stimulate for them, this would be wrong. Allow them to walk their own paths with a hand to hold if they require it.

We see now many New Agers cultivating great innovative thoughts on how to educate these new souls. They do not require education – only guidance within the spiritual realms. Their creative minds have been educated. It is now required that this creativity is allowed to have space, and cultivation will occur. When you cultivate your plants you do not try to inspire them to one growth or another; you allow them to spring forth from the seed. Even within your cultivation units of hybrids, once the seed is planted, it is allowed to grow comfortably.

More time will be given to educating the children at some other time, but we warn now of too much conforming and organising. Organisation has many areas where it will lead you to greater things, but in the area of children it will only lead to mutation and negligence. Negligence of the needs of the soul will be another way that you will produce mutants. You are all mutations of the Source. We do not require that you again take this road. Through spiritual experience and understanding you can lead these children into the new age. Do not attempt to accept any of the old concepts of education; they are all outmoded and unsuitable. We will be producing many manuscripts for you on 'education'.

We continue now with the energy transference contact. We will be giving you exact locations of how and when these new energy activations will be carried out. These energy activations of which we speak are to do with exact points, which when activated will begin to spurt energy along the lines and into the main energy supply.

The lines of which we speak are the lines of energy travelling within the area of the Earth. Much has been speculated about these particular lines. We do not accept that your speculations hold much credence. It has become very popular to speak of energy lines within the Earth. These lines have many different aspects of which you do not speak or speculate. These particular aspects are the aspects of dimension and circular diameter. We have attempted many times to make this known to you, but always there has been some great negative impulse which stops the information from being received.

We will now attempt to give you these dimensional and circular aspects. The circular aspect is one which holds great importance. In some cases the lines have become somewhat curved, they do not now hold the circular shape. We must realign and charge these lines in order for the system of energy to hold its power. The energy between the lines will double and cause great masses of land to go into upheaval if this is not completed. Between the lines of energy are landmasses which respond now to other systems of energy exchange. If the lines themselves were in complete working order then this would not happen. Much of the land between lines corresponds now to the ecological system of the land more than to the energy.

We will be suggesting to you that if you go to these places, you must be aware of the damage that has already occurred. In particular areas energy is escaping around the lines and burrowing downwards into the Earth's mantle. Much of this escape will cause dysfunction for the interior of the planet. Her interior is her saving grace, it is her soul's home. The power stored within the interior of the planet will serve as her channel of energy in order for the rebirth to take place. She is not just a dead crust: her interior has the power to change her completely.

The first activations will be in the regions of Israel. She will be the first country to receive the energy of the Creator. It has been written, and it will be seen to be done. Much of her energy has been badly affected by the wars and the battlefields of human conflict. The Earth energy will not survive much longer. Along the lines are activation points. These are now completely available to us, ready for activation. We will as you say 'push the button'. This is not nuclear: it is very clear white light energy which will pulse through these lines and begin the cleansing of the planet's earth structure. We must differentiate here between the energy lines within the stratosphere and atmosphere and the lines of the Earth's solid mass. The lines of activation from the stratosphere and atmosphere are the hologramic designs of which we have previously spoken. We are now giving you information of the lines of activation within the earth-mass. There are various points within the country of Israel which will be activated.

Qu: How many points are there in Israel?
There are thirteen main activation points. They are positioned around the town areas, as all energy lines attract people to them.

Qu: Can you clarify that my understanding is correct that the land energy lines are activated after the energy activation within the hologram vortices?
Yes, the Earth will not respond unless the energy vortices are charged. When they are charged the Earth activation points will begin to come alive. Shortly after this the main energy lines will begin to govern the Earth again. Many have tried to activate these points, but they will not activate until the main energy grid lines are again recharged. You have much confusion upon your planet on the subject of both grids and lines. You do not have enough information. When you answer our call now we will give you the full spectrum of notes that you require to understand just how your planet functions. Your intellects are somewhat more subdued now. We are able to impart much more real knowledge to you.

It is time to begin to understand just how your planet adjusts herself to the in and outflow of energies. The energy that has been present upon your planet has caused many different problems. The main one being that of decadent behaviour. This decadent behaviour is brought about by the energies of the Earth and the vibrational energies around the planet being severely out of alignment with the spiritual energies. For many centuries your planet has suffered much pollution and much warlike behaviour. This in turn has brought much dissatisfaction to the people. The accumulation of negative energy enables this state of affairs to carry on. It is only now that the 'table has turned'. It will be in seven years' time that the energy balance has completely renewed itself. Within this seven-year period the energies within the Earth will be totally aligned to the Master rays. Also the energies that are contained around the planet will have aligned to the Masters. Our mission has been to enable this to be carried out. We can no longer watch as your planet looms towards disaster. This disaster would affect too many other planets and stars. We will not allow this to happen. We will be giving you complete breakdowns of the universal energy system. This cannot be done before time. We await the time when more people are awakened. The universal system does not become affected when there are more people aligned to its source. This source is of the purest nature. It does not destroy or impede on any level. We cannot be persuaded to give you more power until you are aligned to this energy source.

After the change of energy supply in June of this year, you will begin to experience more of a connection to the universal system. The effects of this will be somewhat confusing to those who are still very much asleep. They will not believe what they are experiencing; they will not be integrated. We will endeavour to give you some warning of what to do when this energy is activated. It will be as if a storm has hit the planet. Much of the atmosphere will become enlivened with small particles of energy. These particles have some-what of a disturbing effect when approached from a logical point of understanding. They cannot be logically understood.

Any of you that have begun to receive our contact will not make great issues of this, but there will be scientists who do not in any way begin to understand what has happened. The energy will be explo-sive. It will be as if the sons of God have arrived. Many who have been waiting for ascension will ascend. It will be in groups. Ascen-sion is the beginning of the next stage of your growth cycle. There will be approximately 200,000 individuals who will attain this state. We are very excited about this event. It heralds the beginning of the New Age. Very soon after this many more will ascend. There have been many new arrivals. New arrivals that have, over the last couple of years awakened, moved at an enormous pace towards this ascen-

sion process. Many of the new arrivals have been catalysed by the
first-wavers, those who will go first. It is as if there has been a
spiritual revolution upon your planet. We wish to congratulate those
who have been able to release themselves from the material and
emotional fields of influence. They have surpassed themselves
greatly.

Before we give more of the actual earth movements, we must add
that there are still many who do not reach for this state. Do not
become complacent upon the earth plane. You have not as yet
reached your destinations. Along the way are many tests, some will
be extremely painful, others will be somewhat more pleasurable, but
still exacting for those who must pass them. Do not be afraid to
acclaim yourselves as star-seeded. We are in desperate need of those
star-seeded ones to make themselves more obvious. They are still
hiding behind the coverings of espionage. We would be grateful for
more direct contact with these people. They do not do themselves
justice when they are only interested in receiving information
through another.

We would also be grateful for direct communication with all of you
who would like to ascend. We cannot prepare the way through for
you if you are not in direct contact with us. Please put your hands up
and say that you would like to be in contact with us. As usual we do
not try to infiltrate where we are not asked. There are a few occasions
when we are allowed to come unasked into somebody's energy field,
but these are few and far between. It would be a very important
occasion when we would be asked to descend into another with no
prior request from themselves.

When the energy activation is over, we will begin at once to
activate the lines within the Earth. We are giving you over and over
the same information in slightly different words, so that you do not
misunderstand our message. We are aware that this information is
brand new and can be misunderstood. We do not wish you to spend
hours attempting to understand but, if you hear the same message
over and over, you will know that it is correct. You do not need to
understand.

Through direct communication we have been able to send this

message through many different channels. This way it will be heard over and over in slightly different forms. But always the same message of the salvation of the planet Earth. You will not hear any different messages come from this area of the Universe. The area in which we reside is the holiest of places. It does not 'rock and roll' as do your vibrations on planet Earth. We contemplate the higher energies. We breathe them in and allow these energies to control our thoughts and actions. We are very much as you are in spirit, but we have had enough of the more basic types of entertainment. We do not look forward to strife. We know only peace and happiness. We would not choose to inhabit your planet at this time.

As time goes by there will be much unleashing of negative powers from those who have allowed their egos to control them. We cannot be responsible for the negative actions that will befall your planet from those who are still totally engrossed in their own power.

There is a two-fold effect which will descend upon the planet Earth. Those who are able to respond will respond faster and more deliberately, but those who are far beyond this type of response will begin to dig deeper ditches for themselves. They must survive somehow, so they will begin to react on a survival level. One of the most basic instincts that mankind has is his own survival. Without the spiritual mantle this instinct becomes highly dangerous. It is without care and concern for others, a primordial fear of extinction. We would be better rid of these types of people, but this cannot be done. The time will come when you walk hand-in-hand with evil upon your planet. We cannot allow this to take control, but it will walk again. There are many governmental powers that have the capacity to explode nuclear bombs which will completely obliterate life on the planet. This will not be allowed to happen. But nevertheless there will be some who contemplate attack.

You can see now perhaps that the information we are giving must be given to those who can respond. Do not attempt to discriminate as to those who will and will not awaken. You cannot always be sure that you are choosing correctly. We will give you all the information you require. It is your responsibility to ensure that all of those who can read will be given access to this material. If it is not responded to it will cause no harm, but if there is no material to read then this will cause much dissent.

For some time now we have been aware of the awkwardness of the gait of the planet. She will not be very far from calamity when these energies are activated in order to balance her. She will be anchored at this time by the energies that are connected to the souls of the beings that have arisen from their sleeping state. We would suggest also that you all take a conscious part in this rebirth. We can and will use the energies of all of those who have raised their vibrations, but we will be best served by those of you who consciously choose to take part in the evolution of your world.

As always we cannot command a response, but we ask you from our hearts to take part in the biggest command performance you have ever experienced. It is not from your royal family that this is commanded, but from your Mother/Father God. We are only pawns in the performance. Our command performance is to give you as much assistance as we can. We cannot activate the energies without the permission of God. Do you understand now that we come as friends of the Universe, not as tellers of bad news?

We will be showing you just how much interference there has been within the energy system of the Earth planet. She does not activate now from her own energy source, but from the negative powers that have been used within the world during the last decade. Her power system has become defunct. It will only be when we activate the hologram energy system surrounding the planet that she is able to power herself again. As soon as she is empowered, she will begin the cleansing.

Much has been changed since man has used the nuclear energy supply. We cannot emphasise enough the negativity that is unleashed when this power source is used. It is because of the activation of molecules and atoms that this power source has a completely negative action. We do not apologise for using such extreme caution to you on this subject. You are unaware of the damage that it is doing to the frequencies and to the universal energy system. We are at liberty to say here that the damage to the universal energy system is at present minor, for you are not totally connected to this system, but we will not allow any more damage to be carried out.

It is at this point that we have needed to carry out the realignment in order for the universal system to remain whole and intact. You cannot trespass on universal territory without extreme penance. We have warned your governments and your scientists; they have not heeded our warnings. There are many manuscripts which give exact details of these warnings – they have not been published. We will warn again, this time our warnings must be heeded.

Before too long you will experience a complete changeover from the avenues of the scientific fields. They will begin to understand just how much nuclear energy compromises the other energies present. It has been a long time since the first experiments. They are now adjusting their findings to include all of the data that has been discovered. Before, they were trying to hide certain factors, and also they were not really understanding some of their own findings. It is because of the change in attitude that we will be allowed to build more energy and power and use this in our activations. If we were not sure that some of these experiments would cease then we would have to use great caution in activating the more powerful energy forces.

We can now proceed wholeheartedly with the cleansing process. We will be in the main unhindered in our endeavours, but nevertheless the cleansing is still very necessary. Nuclear energy fields do not just disappear; they remain very much a part of the atmosphere and stratosphere. The lines of energy surrounding your planet have become severely damaged by this infiltration. For some time now energy has been escaping along some of these lines. Your weather system has been very much a victim to this, also the energy available to your world.

We will allow you to know of all compromises that have been allowed to fester upon the earth planes. You have not been controlling the outcome of many of the disastrous experiments that have been dabbled with. There is much germ infestation within the atmosphere of the Earth. This must also be cleared. These germs were not present when the Earth began. We will be clearing any negative life forms that are present, including those individuals who will not submit to their spiritual mantles.

We do not jest. There are life forms that are not seen with the naked eye. Some are minute, others exist purely within the astral realms, but nevertheless will be cleansed. Apart from these life forms we will also be cleansing every form of substance that does not support the life system of the Earth planet herself. We speak now of chemicals, fertilisers and any other monstrosities that have been used within your world life-support system. It is incongruous to us how you could believe that these substances could support you when they indeed work totally against the life support system of the planet. You do not seem to understand that to support your own lives you must also be in complete unity with what will support the life system of the planet.

Very soon, many will gather upon the Earth plane to unite the planet with mankind. There will be a ceremony which will be performed within the next eighteen months which will begin the uniting of energies between the soul of mankind and the energy system of the planet Earth. Many will gather together, it will come at a time when everything has been revealed. We reveal first in words and then in action.

Do not wait for the action to catalyse you into response. Begin now to readmit the energy field of the planet Earth into your consciousness. She has been in remorse and grief. She does not appeal to your emotions, but to the love that lies hidden in your hearts. Do not be sorry for the deeds already done. Activate your hearts into action now. She needs your love not your fear. If you remain in fear you will allow her energies to subside even further into remorse. After the energising of the earth lines within the physical structure of the planet will come the cleansing of the waterways.

PART THREE

Chapter 14.

The Beginning of the Cleansing of the Oceans and Waterways

We will be clearing the debris from the water system within the structure of the Earth planet after the onslaught of physical change within the Earth structure. We cannot adjust this system when everything is in turmoil.

The energy of the water will be altered. It is at the moment completely hydrogen based. It will become both hydrogen and methane. The energy of the methane will allow any 'objects' that are lodged in the energy of the hydrogen to be released. This methane energy will be immersed into the supply because of the great traumatic movements of earth-mass.

You will presuppose that anything on this scale would have to be controlled. Nature will control herself. She has the ability to operate within any traumatic situation and still remain true. We do not wish you to even consider how to cleanse the waterways and seas until this operation has been successfully completed.

Nature will control the seas and waterways by combining these two energies. What will actually occur is that the energy of the hydrogen will be cleansed on a molecular and atomic level. We cannot give you exact equations here, but you will be able to experiment yourselves by immersing methane into hydrogen compounds.

Do not attempt to activate any of the cleansing materials that you will still have in supply within the earth plane. These chemicals will again upset the balance of the energies. Do not attempt to counteract with any agents that are supposedly separation agents. These will not work; the separation of debris from water will occur naturally.

We would suggest that, at a later stage, much later, you acquire great sulphur blocks which will help to activate the natural qualities of a cleansing action. These sulphur blocks will be used combined with the rods of carbon dioxide, which together will increase the activity of the green algae within these waterways. It is the combination of sulphur and carbon dioxide which will help to clear and maintain growth. Energies within the water will be different for some time. You will not have enough to eat yourselves, but cannot resort to exploiting the oceans at this time, for they will not be in a condition that will feed you healthily.

We suggest that at this moment in time you become aware of the functions of your own digestive system. This system was designed only for the consumption of healthy green leaves, grains and fruits. It does not make good use of all of the energised and decomposed substances that you inject into it. For some of you it has become a time of fasting and cleansing. This will serve you well as you enter into the next phase of our plan. By the time the negative energy releases are upon you, you will be strong enough to cope with any dietary changes that will be necessary. Fasting now will strengthen the digestive tract. You will be cleansing out any unwanted toxins and bacteria. After the cleansing, be careful not to overload the digestive tract. It will need gentle handling for a time. Be careful that you do not overstress the digestive system at this time.

Many are becoming confused as to which foods to eat. Eating is only a way of sustaining the actual bodily parts. You do not need to eat large amounts of anything. Intuit yourselves what will serve the highest development of your body. It is much better to eat lightly and more often than to overload the system at one time. Be careful not to overload any part of your system. Your digestive system needs to be treated with respect. It has a large part to play in preparing you for the coming years. You cannot survive without sustenance, but in the next few years your sustenance will become very scarce. We warn you now so that you do not suffer too greatly when you are unable to eat those things that you are used to. Become simple in your eating habits; it will serve you well.

Our connection to the medium has been very much easier since she has changed her eating habits. The body is lighter and contact is made easier by the finer energies that are available to us. We are not trying to educate you solely on food habits, but on all the habits that you have held on to in your lifetimes. It is not just one lifetime that harbours many of these habits. You have experienced again and again some of the lessons, but are still holding on to 'what you know can't hurt you'. Well, it can and it does. You only hold on because you are afraid to change. Do not despair, we are here to advise you now. Trust in us. Hold onto our hands; we are leading you to the 'garden of Eden'. You have always wished that life on Earth was easier; we are here to make it so. Do not be wasteful of your time and energy. Learn with us now; it is the only way to the other side.

We will be giving you much information on the oceans and waterways, but must insist that you do not try to coerce your scientists too soon. We will be giving much information to those scientists who are able to listen to us. They do not respond immediately to anything we have to say. But as in their experiments they ponder, they watch, they think and then they surrender.

As usual we will be allowing you to make your own choices, but we must warn you that when you make your choices, take into consideration the movements that are given to you from your hearts. Your hearts will speak to you. It is not always easy to decipher the essence of the truth, but if you allow the movements of your hearts to be heard, you will always make the right decisions.

When your heart speaks it will be soft and caressing. When your mind controls you it will always appear hard and unbending. For the next few months it will be very important that your heart guides you. We do not speak unworthily. We are very much guided by the impulses of the all–powerful heart. It is not in our ability to control anyone or manipulate. We come as the one heart, the impulse of the truth vibrations.

Righteousness will rule again on your planet. It will not come for some time, but from now on the impulse of those who are guided by their hearts will hold the planet on course. There are many who do not understand that of which we speak. Their minds are now so out of control that they have no sense of heart. You must guide these lost souls to seek refuge now in silence and retreat. Through silent retreat they will have the opportunity to regain their sense of self. It will take some time before these lost souls are reunited into the oneness of self, but nevertheless they will return. We speak now of those who will not return. There is a choice to be made.

Many will not return home in this mass exodus. They will choose to remain firmly within the dimensions of the Third Reality. We will not stop them. It is their choice. Do not attempt to use strong forces to convert those who do not wish to be converted. You will begin to realise that there is a difference between the lost souls and the souls who do not realise they are lost. It is the lost ones that will want to hear your words, and join with the energy fields of those who have already found their way.

Very soon the energies will rise again, the vibration will almost be at its highest frequency. This high frequency is one that will command the beginning of the next phase. During this next phase much will change. We are attempting to allow you much more forewarning.

Very soon the energies will subside and recover the lost land masses that have been hidden from your view. Much of the island of the British Isles has been hidden. There are secret pathways along the edges of the cliffs of Dover. These were used many years ago when man was closer to the Earth. He would channel out vast underground caverns when he was being attacked or thwarted in his attempts at a peaceful life. Many caverns have been hidden; these will be revealed.

There is much information that has been secret. Along the edges of the River Thames are secret dugouts which have served well for many a warrior. These again will be utilised when they are required. We ask that you do not attempt to discover any of these. As time goes by you will come across many different areas which have been hidden from view. During the changes much will be revealed. There are secret caverns in nearly every part of the United Kingdom. Do not hesitate to take refuge when there are threats of sabotage from the element of society who will run in fear and greed.

Very soon the energy will return to its balance. During this time much will be accepted. Do not attempt to change our words. We give you exactly the energy required to catalyse those who require it. If we required you to change our words, then we would advise you accordingly. Each word has a vibration and an energy counterbalance. Each word will resonate towards the truth and then open those who are ready to be opened.

For some time now the energy around the east side of the British Isles has been changing. Much is caught up in the middle of the Atlantic Ocean. The energy there will go through a massive clearance. During this clearance it will not be safe on the seas. Do not attempt to enter the seafaring challenge. Many will be thrown overboard and lost at sea during these changes. If you are in any doubt as to the movements that you should take, then ask us directly. We cannot act solely as a travel bureau but we can and will advise you of any mishaps that you may encounter.

For a long time now, energy has been building around the tropics. Many islands are now in the height of energy transference. This will be released very soon. Many of the Caribbean islands will suffer greatly, but as soon as the energy releases then the recovery will also begin.

If you begin to understand that once the energy has begun the releasing process, then peace will also begin to reign; this peace will be intoxicating. For some the energy will bring more and more catastrophe. It is only those who do not surrender that will feel the need to criticise what is going on. Those who surrender will breathe in the new vibrations and feel more and more at ease. The ease will be felt within your very bones. You will know that you are returning home, home to the finer and more easily accessible waves of love. Along the way many will become angry and create much chaos as their homes and loved ones are lost. Do not become entangled in this sort of scenario. You are not of this world; you come from many different planets which do not revel in discord and emotional despair. Right action will be carried out on your planet Earth.

The waterways will suffer greatly, they are even now under much stress and pollution. Do not attempt to begin the cleansing until the changes have ceased. The natural process which will be carried out for you will cause much of the sediment to settle. The finer cleansing will be something that you will become involved in much later. As time goes by you will begin to understand that the waterways cannot

be controlled. They have their own natures, both physically and
spiritually. We do not wish you to control Nature. Nature can guide
and inspire you if you allow her. She has been in control for much,
much longer than mankind. It is only during the last few centuries
that man has tampered with and manipulated Nature. Now you will
reap the results of your meddling.

For some, there will be a great involvement in Nature. Many will
again reach for the natural habitats, the natural laws and allow Nature
to guide them back to a basic lifestyle. These will be the ones that will
instruct the governments on how to build a lifestyle which is in
balance with Nature.

Water and energy are the two elements which will serve the basic
requirements of mankind. Energy is the first element. Everything is
built within the fields of energy. Water has many different forms:
some would be classed as solid and physical, and others as sublime.
Do not interfere with the element of water. We can offer you many
suggestions as to how to obtain the water that you will require, but
we do not wish you to corrupt any of the waterways or streams.
Oceans have never been your servants and will not now be so. If you
begin to see each ocean, each waterway or stream follows the course
that Nature creates for it. It does not always make sense to your
logical minds, but is nevertheless perfect in its creation. If we were to
attempt to work against Nature then our world would also become
polluted and at risk. We do not work against any of the creative
principles. Nature is the creative principle of the environment. She
does not require any changes.

We wish you now to become like elves playing in your playing
fields, dancing within the principles of Nature. You are spirits of the
world. Do not chain yourselves to inventions and technological disasters. You were given the opportunity to be happy in your environment. You were not satisfied and have tried many different paths of
distraction. Do you wish now to be happy and at ease with the way
things were? We will ask again and again.

Many will begin to ask themselves this question. If happiness is a
gift of God, then surely you must walk hand in hand with God in
order to receive this gift. This gift is now available to you all, it is as if

a great amnesty has been granted and now you must raise your hand if you wish to participate.

All sins will be forgiven. This great amnesty began two thousand years ago, but was not taken as an amnesty. Many fought to overrule the power of the Christ spirit. Now the time has come to accept amnesty. You have all sinned, but have gained much experience within these earthly planes. You do not need to stay in sin any longer. The Christ spirit is here on Earth and will now heal the sick and the lame. We do not speak of physical sickness and lameness, but of crippled spirituality and sickness.

You have all gained many things while playing the game of 'life'. Now it is time to play the game of reality.

Chapter 15.

We will begin now with the rest of the synopsis of the waterways. During the oncoming changes many of the rivers will become water-logged. This will require some management, but not drastic manip-ulation of the system. We do not wish you to dam any of these rivers. The excess water should be drained off, but not allowed to accumu-late at any one point. When the rivers are dammed, they do not flow free. The energy of the river is then severely affected. If the excess water is drained off, then the energy will not be affected.

We would suggest that each river is monitored for extreme build-ups of water. In this way you will be assisting the passage of the water, not causing it harm. When a river overflows, it is allowing the excess to drain off. It is a simple equation; when anything is filled to excess, the extra will need to be siphoned away.

Nature has her own ways of adapting to sudden changes. Can you also adapt? We are aware that you have used many of the drainage areas of the waterways for your habitats. Now is the time to change your habitats. You cannot use these overflow areas for safe habita-tion. It is incongruous to us as to why this would be thought of as a good idea. It is never a good idea to try to readjust Nature. You cannot expect to be safely housed when you are on very unsafe territory. Choose your habitats according to the flow of the land and the balance of earth energies. Do not attempt to infiltrate into Na-ture's own chosen grounds for river overflow. If she has chosen to flow water in a particular area, there will be a subsidiary area around this which is also her territory. You have much space on your Earth planet that could have been utilised. Now is the time to begin the process of relocation. If you do not adjust, then Nature will adjust you.

For many there will be much trauma and stress when they realise the extent to which the oceans and waterways will be affected. This will come too late for many. They are not able to readjust, and will remain firmly seated in their places of familiarity. We cannot always keep the safety of the people in these areas. It is only through awakening and realising that the higher energies are not controllable, that many will see the light of the new day. It is an uncontrollable force that is upon your planet. We cannot control the energies. We too are only pawns within the totality of the complete divine plan. It is an ingenious plan. One that will not be surpassed.

During the energising, much of the water has been affected. It is not just energised, but now contains many different molecules. Some are healthy, others are not. The combination of stress, from the negative elements present already in the water and the higher frequencies, carries out its own molecular and chemical changes. This will be subdued in time, but must carry out the whole process of metamorphosis. If you begin to adulterate this water with yet more chemicals and cleansing agents, you will be upsetting the natural cleansing action.

For some time now much of the energy releasing from the oceans and the waterways has been somewhat concave. We are trying to give you some sort of idea of the complexity of the system of energy stimulation. It is not enough to begin to understand the complexity of the water system itself, but you must begin to understand the energies that are governing this system. In every part of the world the energy of water has become concave. Concave energy has the energy particles in reverse. When the energy system has been cleansed this will revert back to its original pattern.

Patterning of energy was conceived originally when the divine plan of creation began. Before mankind became the inhabitant of the Earth planet, much was different. It is because of the thought patterns and emotional degradation that energy has been adulterated. Every thought and every emotion will have its effect on the environment. Your thoughts are based on a coding of energy frequency. Your emotions are bound by energy frequency. We will adjust these frequencies so that the original patterning returns.

For some time now energy has been reversing. This reversal of components has resulted in the increase in energy build-up. We will attempt to give you many more formulae for decoding the system of energy. It is not a simple task. Each energy particle has trillions of energy molecules. Each molecule can be split again and again. We speak to you now of the dynamics of physics.

Before too long the physicists who are expanding their knowledge of the Universe will discover just how far they are away from the real understanding. They have become rigid within their minds and this rigidity will be ripped away as more and more phenomena are discovered. It will be a time of remorse and a time of renewal. The remorse will be because of the long time period which has been lost in analysis, and logic which has been wasted. For some there will be discoveries which will blow away the myths and equations which have for so long supported the system of physics.

The waterways carry vast amounts of water and waste. Every energy particle is affected by the waste products. It is not usual for the energy of water to be polluted and mutilated. Can you begin to see that the waste products do not cause the system to completely adulterate? If the energy of water was pure, then the breakdown would not be so complete. It is the particles of energy that have become the major problem. You are not looking at the breakdown of the water content; your scientists and politicians only examine the physicality of the water. If we do not change the energy then the water will remain 'polluted'. None of the cleansing agents can change the energy particles within the water system.

We are attempting to expand your consciousness so that you are aware of the energy system within everything on your planet Earth. She is a system of complex energies. Do not attempt to analyse the conditions within the Earth planet without first understanding that she is controlled by energy. If the energy is mutilated, then you will never understand the conditions that prevail. First and foremost the consciousness must now begin to accept the presence of the energies. You will find it easier to understand if you first look at the system of structure.

Within the building industry, there is first a drawing or blueprint, then come the foundations and then the structure. The drawing or blueprint is also present within the water. Each water particle has its own blueprint. It also contains a foundation and then a physical structure. Each particle will operate separately. If your buildings were built with weak materials, the walls would collapse and the ceilings would not hold the weight of people walking on them. The pipes would burst and the electrics would fuse.

This system is causing the waterways to burst their banks, the streams to build excess negative pollutants. But before the physical effects are felt the blueprint must have become adulterated. This blueprint contains the energy. Within the building industry the energy is implanted by the creative impulses of the architects concerned. If we begin to look at the blueprint from the waterways, this was constructed by a Master Builder, one who did not expect that his energy would be adulterated – that his master creation would be thought lacking and then changed beyond recognition.

Very soon you will understand that to honour and obey the creative principle is one of the most important laws that will return to this planet. You have many rules and regulations, man-made. When you begin to return to the laws of the Universe you will have made your peace with your maker.

If we are to instruct the societies that will inhabit the planet Earth in the future then our emphasis will be purely on universal law. The law of the one. We are now beginning to give you more of the understanding that you will require in order to rebuild a lifestyle that will support you and support the supporter – Mother Earth. This life-support system is one that can perpetuate a feeling of ease. Dis-ease will not be part of this new life support system. It has no place.

The Earth will expand her consciousness as you expand yours. She has been for many centuries caught in a negative energy field. When this has released, her spirit will soar and her energies will rise to the frequency she has known before. Do not try to hold her back. For many centuries her energies have been forced to stagnate and hold negative impulses. It will be like a new dawning, a new energy. When everything upon your planet is operating from the laws of the

Universe, then you will hold the dawning of the New Age.

Throughout time there has always been an impulse which has never died. Every one of you knows of this impulse. Some are now rekindling their feelings for the impulse. A pulsating light was given to you. You will never forget completely what this light is and where it comes from. Do not try to remember for fear of forgetting. If you attempt to remember, you will forget. We do not want you to forget. You will only realign with the light by going towards it. It does not require any intellectual understanding. This may appear ambiguous, but we wish you to trust and surrender to the light not understand where it comes from. It is something that every one of you knows. Before long there will be many who will realign with this light. The light comes from the universal source of all energy.

Understanding does not bring enlightenment. Enlightenment is to be at one with the light. It is beyond your intellects. If we were to show you how the light can permeate through your very beings, then you would understand but first we must have complete surrender. It is the equation of know thyself and know the Creator. For some this is too simple: they wish to know everything but themselves. If you continue on the pathway of understanding how everything within your universe operates, then you will be tied up in conflict. Surrender to the light of the Universe and everything will be revealed.

We would like to approach now the topic of industrialisation. This subject has been one that has been addressed many many times. We are now attempting to address this subject in a spiritualised fashion.

Many of you are aware now of the overstimulation of this element of your society. It is because of this that you are now approaching the cataclysmic situation on your planet Earth. Very soon the industrialisation programme will be defunct. It will become defunct because of the over-active zealousness that has been involved during the last decade. You cannot over-activate and then expect the system to carry the balance that is required. When things are over-active there then becomes the time of non-activity. It will almost become totally silent.

During this period there will be much development of minds and consciousness, not in a purely logical way, but in a spiritual manner. Very soon you will see the re-emergence of an industrialised section of your world, but this will become very much in line with the cosmic consciousness.

You cannot support a nation with money, but there will be a need to re-establish community profits. The form that these profits take will be much more along the lines of a barter system. Each participant will be encouraged to develop their own talents and gifts. In this way many will be supported.

In every society there has always been the need to create a system of pay and earn. In the past this system has become corrupt. We are going to assist you in creating the best system that supports not only your creativity, but your spirituality.

It will appear as if nobody needs to 'work'. In fact nobody will be working in the way that you have understood this word. Work can only be productive when it comes from the heart. Each person has the capacity to 'earn' their keep by being just themselves in each and every way. Each one of you has the capacity to be yourself. We will be assisting you on your passage into the new order. This new order does not require the assistance of great mathematical formulae or great escapades in society structure. The essence of your being is the only requirement for the new order to come into being. Each one of you has this essence.

It will be as if a great hole has opened up within the spectrum of logical thinking. You cannot think yourselves into peace and happiness. Peace and happiness will occur as each and every one of you communicates directly with the higher octave of your vibration. Each vibrational movement will bring you closer to the end result – your utopia. Our utopia has many more octaves within its capacity than that of the earth vibrations.

Each one of us has the capacity to grow further. We are attuned to the highest vibration of which we are capable within the 'time' span allotted to us on this frequency. Our frequency has many facets. We do not look for results, but only growth. It is a frequency of expansion and materialisation. This materialisation has been very much misunderstood from the areas of your earth plane. We can materialise what we require, but do not need to compete with our requirements. We require only materials and substances in order to grow.

Our needs are not our desires. Desires would submit us to the realms of Third dimensional existence. Before very long you too will experience a need to obtain certain 'things', but you will not then acquire anything that does not serve the purpose of your requirements. When we are communicating through our channel we are attempting to use words that we cannot extract from within her vocabulary. We have many thoughts which do not match with the way in which you have constructed the language that you use. Our ways are not your ways. Our language is not therefore available always through the vocabulary that we have at our disposal.

Many people are already understanding that before too long there will be no system of central government. During this time you will be relying on what you know and how you can manage to handle any given crisis without being directed by governmental bodies. Each one of you, if you rely on your higher knowledge, can handle any of these crises. We are calling them 'crises' because of the way that you at the moment will respond to them. As you approach the time of great changes you will find that you do not then refer to them as disaster areas or crises . Many will flee from any changes. They will be fraught with panic and fear, anger also. This anger can be dissipated if only they would pray to God for forgiveness. You cannot change the unchangeable. We would like to be able to give all of you the faith and trust.

Because of the indiscretions upon the earth plane there will many who do not wish to become enlightened. It is as if the indiscretions have become like addictive pills holding you into a bondage of malpractice. When one allows just a little of the light to shine on you, then it becomes more difficult to practice indiscretions. Each particle of light shines on the more decadent parts of yourself and reveals them to you. You can no longer stay unconscious as to your indiscretions. As your saying goes 'it is ok, as long as you do not realise just how black the kettle is when it calls the pot black'. But when you realise just how much blackness there is in yourself, you no longer can call anyone else black, for you realise the hypocrisy.

Very soon there will be a vacuum created, whereby nobody can move any further on, until the energy contained within their own energy lines has cleared to an extent whereby the frequency of higher vibration can enter. We do not infer here that many will stop developing, but only that there will come a time when the vibrational frequency cannot come and go, but must remain fixed within your systems.

In order for this energy to be allowed to stay constantly within your bodies, you must have erased many of the past patterns and complex inferiority syndromes. If you feel inferior, then you cannot become superhumans. Many of you feel the need to compensate for your lacks and doubts. Do not be afraid now to own your personal freedom, own your courage, own your abilities. For many this will be difficult; there has been much programming of 'one should not be in praise of oneself'. We do not advocate pride and arrogance, only praise of the super beings that you are and will activate within this world on Earth.

For us it is a different world, our world does not contain humanoid dysfunctions; we do not battle with your diseases, your energy imbalances. Can you imagine how easy it will be to progress consciously and spiritually when you do not have to wonder how you feel or whether your body can handle the energy? There has been much correction of bodily functioning over the last decade, but because of the energy levels that are ascending to your planet Earth, you are again needing to balance the physical body.

We have been assisting many of your researchers, many of your surgeons and doctors. They are beginning to respond. There are some that are now able to see that the DNA has changed. As with much of the secret information within your Earth world, this will not be openly revealed, but we are aware that the changes within this section of your system have begun. We will activate within every section of your system. Each system of organisation will require a certain degree of activation. We cannot always stay and follow through because of the decree of 'do not command', but we are allowed to begin the first activation process.

Many have been surprised themselves at suddenly 'seeing through' the years of research that they have carried out, and inexplicably sensing the solution. We sense here that you know we are able to chuckle at the attitudes of your scientists and researchers. They have been staring the answers in the face for years, but do not allow their senses to answer for them. If they were to carry on in the same old logical fashion, with their truths and untruths, I am afraid your planet will self-erupt before the experiments can be finished.

Some of the ideas that have been researched have failed to result in any kind of solutions, because of the logical viewpoint of the scientists and researchers. If they were now to view the same experiments with much more of their intuition, then they would be given all of the answers. There are no experiments which cannot offer answers when given the whole spectrum of insight. We are baffled by the incompetence of your so-called experts. They have only eyes for the obvious. If they were to look behind the obvious, all of the answers would be there for them to see. If we were to observe the universal system with blinkered eyes then we would not understand or even experience what there is to experience.

It is only through breadth and depth of vision and insight that any of you will be able to comprehend the energies and the energy system. It is not complicated, it is however very much simpler than anything you will attempt to pursue. This is not the simplest pathway to walk. You do not accept simplicity; you will always look for the most complicated theories and explanations. We have a need to expand your thinking, but not expand your logic. It may seem an impossible task, but we can and will expand your consciousness in order to activate the workings of your creative mind. This creative mind will need to expand greatly.

There are many who are finding that their minds do not function very well. It is not that you are having difficulties, but that there has been a disjointed approach before and you are not used to using the more creative functions of your mind. It will appear as if you are losing the function of long-term memory and indeed some of the short-term memory. This memory has not been lost, but has now been placed much more within the back quarters of your mind. For the creative mind to begin working fully, there is a need to balance the logical side into a more equal partnership. This partnership of left and right brain working together will ensure that you do not run amok with the crazy ideas of advancement and technology without first addressing the consequences of cosmic awareness. We do not require you to become robots. The main plan involves the evolvement of man within a very short space of time. If we left you to evolve without our conscious involvement, you would indeed be only a short span of time away from complete obliteration.

There are some of your main researchers within the sections of the scientific world that are definitely delaying the process of evolution. There are facts that have been researched and realised many years ago that are not given to the man in the street. Their fears are mainly responsible for this deceit. If we can remove the fear then there will be an upsurge in information and understanding which will enable mankind to grow towards enlightenment.

If you are not given all of the facts, then you can only decide within a restricted perimeter how you feel, and also what you should do. If they were to allow all of the facts to be revealed, it is believed that there would be a panic situation. What they do not realise, yet, is that there will be panic anyway, but only within the sections of the public that do not consider that they are any more than their physical being. It will be the exact same result, both by withholding or giving out the facts. Some will 'know' that it will be ok, and others will panic and respond with fear. If the information had been given when realised, then there would not have been this great delay, the sorting of the chaff from the wheat would have begun much earlier.

You cannot suppress the natural soul evolvement. We do not consider that the information has to be revealed more quickly now, for we have been activating many of you without the help of the so-called scientific revelations. But it is nevertheless very important that at least some of your scientists awaken from their unconscious state. When the time approaches for the world to embrace her new-found planet Earth, then you will require some scientific information on the way to conduct yourselves in the future. If you do not understand some of the simpler equations of survival then you will have difficulties again.

Chapter 16.

The energy that has been held within the waterways system will be released after the cleansing of the earth-mass. We will endeavour to keep you informed at each stage of the releasing. In this way we can ensure that you will always have adequate warning before a particular area is affected by the changes. We will always be present when the Earth cleans her energy field. She does not need our assistance at this time, but we are going to be present in order for the masses of awakened people to be protected. We cannot always assist those who are in fear, but we can and always will support all of those who call on us during times of stress and pain.

One of the most important issues to be dealt with will be that of the oceans. The oceans are very dark and cloudy. The atmosphere and the stratosphere have caused the energy of the oceans to become heavy. When the balance of one part of the system is affected, then many other parts react. This reaction does not appear to have helped your scientists and researchers. It is almost as if they are blind to what they see. We cannot be responsible when all the facts are visible and no-one responds. We will be responsible for the awakening of many, but we can only say here that there will also be many who fail to respond. For some of the fish and oceanic life forms it will be a time of extinction. Many of the smaller fish are already struggling to survive in these dark, dank waters.

When the energy is released from the oceans the fish will be submitted to vast changes. The energy cannot be contained. The dolphins are already in position. The energy of the dolphin has for some time now helped to stabilise. When the energy of the oceans release, the dolphins will swim into these regions. The energy will be absorbed by this remarkable animal. We do not call the dolphin a fish because of its remarkable powers and energy. Many dolphins have already begun the movement towards these areas. Their powers of telepathy are greater than that of man. They have been listening to the vibrations of the planet Earth and the oceans. When one dolphin hears the 'sounds', then these sounds are given to all of those dolphins in the area. In this way they have access to the information resounding around the planet. The contact they have with us is very direct. We do not communicate with the individual dolphin, but with the group energy. Their capacity to respond as the one energy has given them the opportunity to be of great service to the planet. Their energy will balance when needed. They have the capacity to be part of the divine plan. When the information is given to them they do not have to respond on any other level than the spiritual. It is as if they are 'one'.

Some of the life in the oceans needs to be cleansed. Many of the deep water life forms have been around for thousands of years. This level of existence will become extinct. When the oceans have become balanced, the need for some of the smaller marine life will have become obsolete. When the waters are clear there will be a strange silence that seems to emit energies from this water. It will be as if the clear water has become energised. We are aware that many of you do not dare to envisage clear water. When you see clear water, you will begin to realise everything that was known and will be known again. Water is an agent of spiritual upliftment. It carries the energy of Spartacus.

In the far-off regions of space there are many beings who have energised the power of water. Some planets have never experienced the special energies of this element. In time to come you will discover many of the qualities of clear water. Spartacus has many functions, some are due to the quality of the atmosphere within this planetary realm. Others are due to the high vibration to which this planet is aligned. The beings who are present within the 'atmosphere' of Spartacus have very small heads and round bodies. Their vibration does not enable them to travel, but they can nevertheless use their energy.

When water passes through the cosmic system, it has many

changes through which it passes. One of these changes is when it becomes energised by the vibrations of the Spartacan beings. These beings have been seated within this vibration for many thousands of your years. They do not need to be as part of the divine plan in a direct manner, but will nevertheless be playing a part when the energy of water has been recognised by the people on Earth. We do not require you to be of absolute air velocity. There will always be water present upon planet Earth. You must now be responsible for the activation of the energies present in it.

You can use water now as a cleansing agent. It is not so much a physical cleanser, but an energy balancer. Many of the atoms and molecules within the system of water upon your planet have been damaged, but if you insert your whole body in a bath of clear water you will be cleansing not only the physical, but the etheric and astral segments of your being. You cannot always understand our answers, but you will always discover these things for yourselves if you decide to carry out the procedures that we suggest.

Clear water will become very much a symbol of the new order. The new order will understand and create many great edifices of cascading water. Running water will enable you to grow and expand as spiritual beings. It is the energy of the element that is important. Many of you now gather at the great natural running water edifices. You watch and gaze in wonder. When you return from one of these sightseeing adventures, you will have cleansed and rebalanced the entire system of energy that controls your body. Much of what we have to give to you is lost knowledge, you have known all of these things before.

When we speak now of great changes, we speak also of knowledge being reborn. Information has always been available. Some of the best known scientists use the element of water when they are experimenting with different substances. In this way they are confusing the answers. Much of the time the element of water is causing the results that they see. When the energy of water is combined with chemical substances it disintegrates. When the energy of water is combined with natural substances, it causes many of these substances to change.

Can you see that because you do not always take into consideration the energy of water, then you can never completely understand what is going on? Water will always respond, but sometimes in a negative way and sometimes in a complementary fashion. If water does not always contain the same energy particles, then how can these experiments prove the results that are sometimes logged? It is as if we must completely re-educate the majority of your scientific institutions. We will not bother. There are many more important issues to cover and when the frequency of energy is higher they will see for themselves.

When water is taken into your bodies, you are aware that you feel more alert and more in control. This is because the energy of the water is higher than the energy of the physical matter within your bodies. If you do not have enough water in your system, then you become weighted down by the lower frequency of the physical matter. Enough water will enable you to see and hear frequencies that you have not seen or heard before.

If you are unable to respond immediately to this invitation because of skepticism or fear, then by trial and error attempt to take in more water each day. You will see that you will become addicted to water which we might add is something much more positive to be addicted to. You cannot absorb water that has other elements added directly into your energy system. In this way you have become much slower and more sluggish. Many of you are drinking more clear water, but you must now make this a new pattern to adhere to more often. If we could allow you to see us, you would see that we come as friends. Some of you will be able to see us quite soon, those that have raised their vibrations sufficiently will become at 'one' with us. In this way they will be able to communicate with us directly. We await this unity and pray for the day.

There have been many substances used on your planet for different experiences. These have never given you the ultimate experience of joy and happiness. The experiences that we offer now are of this calibre. Do not try to obtain joy and happiness from the physical world. It cannot and will not give you this. It is by using the higher frequencies that you will receive that which you have searched for. Many of you have tried the mind-expanding drugs, have they ever expanded your minds? We can expand your minds every time that you converse with us. You can use our energy to give you peace and expansion.

Tell all of your friends and loved ones when you speak to us. They do not understand until they too have a direct experience, but as you tell them of other things that happen to you, tell them of us. We will support any of the people from your planet Earth if only they would turn towards us.

We cannot impose. We have spoken of the decree many times. Do not blame us if we are not there for you; it is because you did not ask us to be so. Fortunes have been found and lost and will be lost again. The fortune of contacting your spiritual friends will never be lost. You cannot lose something which has become part of yourself.

Many have dabbled within the realms of hypocrisy, they speak of great spiritual lessons and then do not practise what they preach. They too will become lost when the energies become of the highest. We cannot give you exact numbers, but at the moment we are losing many more souls because of this hypocrisy.

Very soon the highest of high will be upon you. You cannot then fight and disagree; it will never be changed that way. For some this will be a time of dispute with their very Maker. We will not make it more difficult for you by giving you more information than you can tolerate, but we will always give you small snippets of the essence. In this way we are activating the codings within your own systems. You have always known that there would be a judgment day, what you did not know was that you would still be able to choose which way to go. We will discuss with you at a later stage, the Maker!

For our close today we will give you a small poem –

There are many flowers within your planet,
Each flower blooms at a different time,
When the blooming occurs,
There are many who delight.
We are not here to give you the blooming time,
You are now all responsible for when you decide
that the time is right.

As you are culminating in your own life patterns, we can see that there are some that do not know how to release themselves. This releasing process involves letting go of the energy that has surrounded these negative patternings. It is only the energy that requires change, not the memory or indeed the actual happenings. There are many different ideas and procedures that are being followed, but the main idea of energy release has not been directly addressed. It is only the energy that requires change.

The procedure that we would suggest you carry out is one of utmost trust and honesty. The honesty is the main factor. The trust is something that you must give in order for the releasing to be complete. Many are stuck within the memories of not only this lifetime, but many lifetimes. In order to release the coding of this lifetime you must now forfeit the memories of other lifetimes. Those lifetimes gave you the experiences that were needed for your growth and evolvement. You do not now need to keep rekindling these experiences. It has been a great part of the New Age movement – these regressive experiences.

We would only suggest that you use these experiments in order to rekindle the lost knowledge from these times, not the emotional turmoil. Much of the emotion is being rekindled. It is not required. We can only give you the skeleton of what is now required. It is up to you to realise just how much of yourselves you can give up in order to rekindle only the spiritual knowledge. For some it has been a pathway of complete ignorance. For some it has been a pathway of correct action. You will need now to give yourselves completely to the path of spiritual alignment.

The energy of all of the experiences that you have had can be released through mind control. During this mind control exercise you must release all of that which does not now serve the spiritual ideology. What is required is the unmasking of the being, the exposure of the soul. The soul does not carry past memories. It has only its own essence. During the times of incarnation upon this earth plane, many have become so encumbered in the worldly dimensions that they have forgotten what in fact the soul is, and no doubt do not know where it resides within themselves. During some of the lifetime experiences you will have discovered a small part of what and who you really are. These are the only memories that you are required to link with. If you are linking in with the vast number of times that you forgot who you were, then this will not assist you, but could in fact take you further into the mire.

During this incarnation you have the opportunity of rekindling your physical self with your soul essence. It will be the only time that this has become possible. It is not because of your great spiritual growth that this is possible, but because the vibrations of your planet Earth are being activated. This activation precipitates the procedure through which you are awakening.

We did not know when we came to you that all of the planet had fallen asleep. When we were given our first instructions for the doom and gloom of the changes, we had felt that it would be our position to place the first cataclysmic energy transferences into the atmosphere, then all would be well. But, because of the sleepiness of your planet the energy has been required again and again. The energy did not catalyse enough of you to encourage the awakening. We have come again and again.

Now the plan is well into its second stage. This stage is one of gigantic proportions. We do not underestimate with these words. It is not just an evolutionary move forward, it is the quantum leap of which some of you speak. This wording will serve you well. Within this wording is coded the explicit energy of the ascension process. We are taking quantum leaps by preparing the way for you to ascend. Our own ascension was carried out in this way, but we are now preparing to ascend many, many individual souls at one time. This is not an easy procedure. It is one that requires great precision and quality.

During the ascension process, some of the souls will rejoin their group souls. This will mean that they do not return to the planet Earth, but will decide to carry on their work within the soul groupings. We cannot give you exact numbers of persons that will take this route, because it is completely an unknown factor until the moment of ascension. Some will return almost immediately. During the period in which they will be given complete freedom of the spiritual mantle they will be away from the planet Earth. We cannot give you the freedom of the spiritual mantle whilst you are still within the realms of the planet Earth.

The energy must be of the highest frequency. During this timespan many will have contact with their Earth bodies. It will be as if there has been a missed day or indeed maybe a few missed hours. The physical body will remain in a comatose state. The breathing will be reduced to a faint whisper and the lungs will not dilate through the oxygenation of the blood. For a period of time, most of the physical capacity of the body will remain inactive. We cannot at this time completely expose all of the details. For some it will become as if they are asleep, for others as if the motion of the physical body has stopped. Do not become afraid, for if you are agreeing to ascend, then you will understand. It will be as if when the moment has arrived you will arrive a moment before it. Complete surrender will occur momentarily. During this moment everything that needs to be accomplished will be so.

From this time on, the energy of the planet Earth will accelerate. This acceleration will cause much of the energy of the negative areas to release. It is only within this releasing that the energy can be balanced.

When we have spoken to you of ascension, we have not been able to completely outline what is about to occur. This has come about because of the total anarchy that would have been allowed to surface if this matter had been spoken of before its time. Some of you are as you say 'well seasoned' with the energies, but many are still opening their eyes for the first time. We could not allow those who were just opening their eyes to be shocked and fall immediately back into sleep. We have chosen well our timing. It has been some time now that the divine plan has been revealed, but only through those that would submit this to the few. We are now ready to give all of the information to the world.

For some it will now be the right time to give information to your press and media functions. Through your links of television and radio much can be accomplished. It is only through mass linkage that we can now reach everyone of the population. Do not feel that this is now for the few, it is for everyone.

We have but a few months left now before the energy will have risen to its full potential. During the time ahead, do not attempt to be a better person. You will only be asked to act according to the 'cut of the cloth'. There will be no rules. When you run, you will run with all your might; do not adjust any of your clothing! We jest with you, but we do not consider that this is really an issue of laughter. We can only be spectactors as we watch how you are still more concerned with your physical appearance than with your spiritual growth!

Very many of the star-seeded ones are now independent. This has been very much a battle of 'what can I leave behind before I begin my mission'. When you are activating your blueprints, there may be no reference to anything that you have taken on board before this activation began. Hence there are many 'things' and 'people' which now do not have any place in your lives. You have lived very much by the 'cut of the cloth that gave you emotional support'. The cut of the cloth has changed; it has no ragged edges, no frayed ends. It is complete – a work of art. You have one position, and that is the one that was given to you before you began the scenarios that have been this first part of your current incarnation.

If you would like, we will give you an analogy, it will be as if you have been alive and then you are reborn. You did not pass through the death phase, but you are nevertheless reborn. Do not be afraid, we cannot always stop you from realising the true wisdoms. If we were to help you to keep yourselves veiled, then we would fail in our attempt to rescue you. A rescuer can only assist someone that is prepared to be rescued. If you were in deep water and could not swim, you would be prepared to be carried across the waves and then swim to shore. We cannot teach you to 'swim', but we will carry you across the waves. You will begin to swim when you realise that you are over the worst of the waves.

Very soon there will be great tidal waves. These waves have the potential of causing much harm and havoc. Do not now spend great amounts of time sitting on beaches and swimming in the oceans. We can only warn you of the approach of these disasters. Do not attempt to be present when one of these waves approaches. We cannot then physically assist you, we can only assist you with the spiritual waves of ascension.

We are afraid that often our words will be taken literally. This has been known before. In your Bible there are many sections that have been used literally, instead of understanding our analogies and stories. When we use the form of 'story telling', we are using a basic idea of archetypal cognitive memory. It is complicated enough to attempt to catalyse those who are sleeping, but we are often faced with misunderstandings of what we are indeed saying; therefore the catalyst does not even break the barrier. Some of the wording has encoded in it very powerful energies. We cannot explain these to you, but will attempt to use them again and again until you are all awake. If you were aware of these key words, then some of you would protect yourselves against them in fear.

There have been some people that have already exposed themselves to the word 'ascension' and have reacted just in this way. You cannot expose yourselves and not be affected at all, but you can certainly begin to put up your barriers. We do not wish to break down your barriers, but only soften them with words with which you can feel safe. There are many words that will be coined now that will be given to all of the people. Some of these words will be given with laughter through the media, but nevertheless they will be given. We do not object when the words are spoken in jest; they are still well and truly spoken. Some of your media chiefs will be working for the good of the planet when they begin to expose just how many of you are going to ascend. They will do this in jest, but as the words are given over the airways, then many more will be activated. Do not underestimate the power of the spoken word.

Chapter 17.

I am going to give you now the information that is required so that the British Isles does not incur more deaths than are necessary. The eastern area of the coast will be awash with tidal waves. The energy that has been building along this coastline has reached a high degree of activation. It will not be long before the energy itself releases and therefore causes much of the ocean to become torrid. The waves that will be upon you are not of small proportion. These waves will mount the beaches and the cliffs. They are bigger than any waves that will have been experienced along this coastline before. We cannot estimate just how much damage will occur, but we are endeavouring to become as a loudspeaker unit which can warn you of these events. You must no longer hold onto any of this information. When the events are upon you, you cannot then say, but we were warned of this. This information must be given to the nation as a whole. Some will take this in jest; others will know that it will be.

Very soon the energies from the oceans will be upon you. Do not hesitate to become part of the network that can give this information to those that will require it. Many of you have been given similar information before, but this has not become common knowledge.

As the energies release, then much of the beach areas and piers will become submerged. For some time there will be water in places where there has never been water before.

Energy does not hold unto itself, it is self-propelling. The actions of energy cannot always be monitored. In this way we are unable to advise you as to the exact distances and timings. But we can give you pre-warning that there will be explosive energies releasing within the oceans.

For some time there have been animals and sea creatures that have been responding to the noise of the ocean and to the energies that are being released. When the energies are building, some of this energy is released prematurely. The sound of the ocean has been changing for some time. She does not resonate with the same tone. The tone has changed because of the energy reversal. Some of the oceans are toned now to a much lower vibration and therefore a lower note. These notes are the notes of energy. They are emitted constantly from the water.

When the frequency of the ocean has been balanced, then you will hear again the music of the spheres. Clear water resonates a crystal clear sound. This sound can emanate vast distances. If you image that the air will be clean and the water will be crystal clear, then you can image also how you too will feel. Everything can resonate on a higher vibrational level.

Clear spring water will give you all of the nutritional aids that you require. Much of the water that is being drunk now on your planet does not contain the minerals and elements that you require within your physical systems. When this water is recycled it does not then remain the pure essence of water; it has become putrefied. When one drinks this water, then the essence of the putrefied matter is still present within the molecules and atoms. Do not drink any of this water. It is much better for you to collect the drops of rain that fall than contaminate your systems with the energy of putrefaction. Clear, cold water will revive your energy systems. It does not require to be heated before the energy will sustain you.

You have become used to many ways of using heat which will not be required within the new order. Heat increases the level of activation within the molecular structure, but this will not give you more energy. It will only disturb your natural balance. You have become used to many substances which do not balance your systems, but agitate them. We will be giving you more facts on what you can eat, and what will severely disturb the system of energy within your bodies. These facts are changing as the time comes close to the energy transference crescendo.

The energy of clear water will become one of the greatest aids on your planet Earth. This will become easy for you to understand as the time approaches when the waterways will become even darker and more dank. During the upheavals, there will be a time when nothing will be quite as before. During this time the energies of water will become severely disturbed. We cannot change what is inevitable, but we are attempting to give you a clear and precise picture of before and after the cataclysmic happenings. If you know that there will be a time when everything will be in reverse, then you will not be shocked and dismayed. If you are also aware that this time will pass, then you can approach the whole scenario with confidence of the dawning of the new day. It will be as if night has turned into day, everything that was bleak and dismal will turn bright and clean.

Energy has the ability to become negative or positively charged. We are endeavouring to show you both the possibilities. If we were only to give you the positive, then you would not survive for you would severely doubt, if indeed this was possible. By addressing the reality of the situation, we can give you hope and faith and trust in the future. It has never helped anyone to look through 'rose-tinted' glasses, but it will give you hope when you see through the eyes of the awakened beings that you are becoming. Do not attempt to give others the rose-tinted view. We are not attempting to give this to you. You would not appreciate us humouring you.

The Earth planet will attempt to gasp and wheeze in order to clear her 'lungs' and clean her reproductive valves. Her valves are the waves of the tidal system. She does not reproduce as you reproduce, but breathes out the new energies in order for her mammals to use this energy. Each new moon, the tidal energies emanate around the planet in order for the souls that wish to incarnate to become immersed within this cycle. For some time now the energies within this cycle have become clogged and much more to do with base sexualilty. During the upheavals the base sexual drive will become almost extinct. It will be a time of celibacy and renunciation.

After the upheavals the time will be given to survival and cleansing. Cleansing on a scale that will be thought of as astronomical. There will be no time for the pleasures of the past, only the pleasures of the present. It will be a pleasure to have survived. It will also be a pleasure to have become in tune with the natural energies of the planet. Many will spend their time bemused by the natural elements of the universal law system. We cannot now give you many of these changes, but we will be in constant contact over the next decade in order to take pleasure with your newfound heaven.

The energy from the oceans will ensure that much of the coastline that needs to be realigned, becomes so. The energies around the inlets of the coastal areas have become very heavy. This is because all energy accumulates, but because of the concave nature of the inlets the energy accumulates more readily in these areas. We are endeavouring to bring about the clearance that is necessary to give you the utmost support. For some time now energy clearance has become necessary. It will be extinct when the new energies rise beyond the normal expectancy levels. What we are attempting to bring about is a situation where negative build-up cannot occur because of the frequency of the energy. Before the sun comes the storm.

For a period of time there will be much devastation and accumulated debris build-up. After this period there will be a time of consolidation and reward. The rewards that are awaiting those who remain within the Earth sphere are beyond any of your wildest dreams. You have not been able to dream of what is to come because of the energy held within the stratosphere and atmosphere of your planet. You cannot go beyond the layers of extreme denseness with your dreaming world. We know that you are expecting a change, but we repeat this will be beyond your wildest dreams. You cannot dream of that of which you do not have a direct experience. You will dream beyond those daily experiences, but cannot reach the higher realms of reality.

When the days of chaos are over you will then be a part of the new energy field. We will not tarry with such notions, because there are far more important aspects of your awakening process that will need to be covered before you reach the peak of your experiences. Abundance will be a major part of your journey through to the higher realms. We speak of abundance of knowledge, abundance of creativity and abundance within your earthly requirements.

Abundance can be found wherever you are situated, when you are in fine atunement with the heavenly hosts. We speak of abundance as

a necessity, as you should not now be concerned with the requirements of the Third dimensional existence, but only concerned with
the requirements that you have in order to complete the tasks that
have been given to you. When we are given an order, we do not have
to become concerned as to where we will find the resources or in fact
the energy to carry this out. We are beyond the realms of need. We
have only to look towards the ultimate goal that we have and we
receive the assistance that is required. Our lives are not controlled by
the fear of lack, for we are truly blessed and gather our inspiration
openly. If we were to imagine that we could not accomplish our
tasks, then we would be in severe doubt as to the source of the orders.
We do not have to work in such a limited way, for we are with the
Father and the Father is with us.

If you were to trust in the Father and the spirit and energy of the
Holy Spirit then you would be as we are, in total and irrevocable
abundance. Abundance will come to you as you relinquish your
desires and begin to join with the strengths of the free passage that
you can enjoy when all has become as one.

There is no separation; there is only choice of movement away
from what keeps you alive. It is as if you are parasites within the earth
plane, only taking and not serving the good of the one. You must
make your passage secure by now joining forces with the energy of
the 'one'. Do not become parasites within the spiritual realms. You
cannot honestly allow anyone to dictate orders to you and not respond from the energy of your own being. This being that you are
will give you all the answers, it has no doubts, no fears. Drop now
any of your images and expectations of being fed constantly from this
decadent, materialistic overview of your planet. It will never give you
the peace and satisfaction that dwells deep within your own soul. You
must rekindle now with your soul and allow the energies of the
Masters to guide you through as you become at one with the very
Moon and stars.

It is not a dream of which we speak. We have said to you that this is
beyond your wildest dreams. Our metaphor does not begin to give
you an insight into the world beyond your world. We have been
intrigued with the insight that has been given to us through working

through some of the mediums. We did not realise that there had been so much re-wrapping around the souls that have been incarnate upon this planet. We have felt as if we have been playing pass the parcel where the wrappers come off and then there are more wrappings. Some are tightly wound around each different chakra, others have pretty bows which say 'I look pretty so please do not let me be changed!' Because of the layers that have needed to be unwrapped, we have been pleasantly surprised when suddenly one of you has torn away many of your own layers, unaided.

We look now for more of you to tear away the last remaining layers in order to be at one with the Universe. You can visualise this process in order to see where you are still covered and how thick this covering is. Within this visualisation process there are keys to the doors. Some of your layers will be covered with very tightly bound plastic. We use an analogy in order for you to imagine just how bound up you can still be.

The plastic-type covering would therefore need to be moved by melting the material, which would entail using the energy of the fire element. If you are dealing with the material of steel, then you would need to incur a great movement through the energy of fracture. This fracture would only occur if you in fact completely abandon yourself to the process of dismantling the blockages.

We are attempting here to give you more precise details of how to deal with these complicated types of coverings that you have placed around yourselves. Each one of you has a completely different spectrum of types of coverings. Each lifetime has given you the opportunity of surrendering or surrounding yourselves with more illusion. As you progress through these lifetimes you have attempted to keep yourselves well within the Third dimensional limits. When you have been tempted by illusion, this has been held into place by certain protective energies which we are now calling wrappings or coverings.

It is sometimes easier for you to understand if we give these energies a physical form. Many are attempting to free themselves, but do not have the wherewithall to do so. It is as if you know of the problem, but do not know which way to dismantle these coverings.

You must first ascertain which type of energy you have used to erect the coverings, then you will have the answer as to which type of energy needs to be used to dismantle them.

We will be giving you many more answers to the questions which we receive in order for these to be given out as general informational guidance encounters. We will also attempt to instruct as many of you as possible in assisting others to now drop this idiosyncratic way of showing others that there are no Masters, only the energy stored within your own beings. If we did not exist, then you would not now be able to be in communication with us.

We have seen that many of the so-called New Agers are beginning to enjoy the energy of their own making so much that they are resorting to condemning the actions of anyone that has surrendered to the hierarchy. This action will not be of any use in the long term. If you do not now surrender you will begin to lose the energy that has been activated. It is only through complete and utter surrender that you will continue to rise within the frequency of energy.

We have seen that some have already begun to slow up and have reached a sort of peak with which they are satisfied. It is now that the great leaps must be made; not complacency of mind and action. There are some that will take the leap ahead of time, but many many others that have now begun to decelerate. We are fearful that the descent of the many will bring about the acceleration of the negative energy releases.

We are dependent upon a great number of you continuing to rise in energy in order for the planet Earth to be held upon the axis when the rebirthing takes place. It is extremely important not to stop at the checkpoints along the way for more than the time it takes you to recover your breath. There are times when it is necessary to breathe and rest, or as you would say 'take a breather', but this does not mean resting for a long period of time and becoming very much one of the 'waders'. Every day now there will be a different time for you to breathe, then walk very quickly along the pathway towards the culmination of the divine plan.

It would be selfish of us to make a great criticism of your actions, but we must continue to assist your passage. We do not criticise, but only come as the bearers of the grace of God. You have been given the grace of guidance throughout all of this plan. We do not assist for our own sakes, but for the sake of life on this your planet Earth. We cannot always address your every need, but can always assist with the appropriate jabs and prods to encourage you to make haste on your own personal journeys. Each jab that we give may appear painful and callous, but we know that we can all rejoice together if we reach the destination on time.

The information that will be given to you concerning the energy of the universal system will now be contained within a separate energised manifesto.

PART FOUR

Chapter 18.

The Passing of the Sun in front of/between the Moon and the Stars

We will begin to now approach the subject of the Sun moving between the Moon and stars. There will be much controversy within this area. We have begun to move amongst those upon your planet that are watching the heavens. We have not as yet been able to secure a direct channelling connection, but we are nevertheless confident that this will occur.

Amongst your astronomers there is one who at this moment cannot understand why there has been so much movement in the regions of the heavens known as the Milky Way. He has attempted to instruct his colleagues on this information, but unfortunately there has been much condemnation. We will be assisting this one to become more in tune with the finer energies of the universal system. In this way he will be able to attune to his own wisdom for he has been in this field many times before.

The energies of the Sun will become very dense after the energies of the planet have been released. For every action there will be a reaction. This is one of the universal laws. We cannot change the energy continuum. We will endeavour to explain to you how the energy of one piece of matter severely affects the energy of another. It is when one energy expands that the energy of another has the opposite effect. When the planet Earth has become re-energised, then the awkwardness of her gait will be corrected. During this correction process the energy of the Sun will be caught within the energy of the planet Earth.

At the moment, upon your Earth you are only concerned with how different actions that are performed outside of your planet will directly or indirectly affect the Earth. What you do not consider is how the energy of the planet Earth has a considerable effect upon all of the other objects in space. Each object will be affected when the Earth goes through her rebirthing process. There will be no planet, solar system, galaxy or solar suns that are not affected in some way. Therefore we will be showing you that when one person raises their arm one inch in one particular area within your planet Earth, then this energy resonates somewhere within the field of gravity. If we look at this on a much larger scale, you will begin to appreciate that every movement that the Earth will make upon her journey will be responded to within each and every galaxy. The areas of your minds have become severely limited during your incarnations upon this earth plane. You have become so finely attuned to the Third dimensional existence, that we are having to almost employ the waves of shock to awaken you.

The energy from the Sun at this time will be averted away from the earth planes in order for the complete task of cleansing to take place. Every time an energy is released from the earth plane, the energy from the Sun would scorch this and increase the velocity a thousandfold. We have needed to deal with this reaction before the energy becomes explosive within the regions of the atmosphere and stratosphere. There is much information which will be given on the complete system of universal energy, which will include much of the data that will be required for you to understand how this process has been addressed, during the compilation of the complete divine plan. We cannot address these issues until we have given you some understanding of how and why the energies have begun to release.

The compilation of the divine plan has been held within the universal continuum for the past 20,000 years. There has been much energy spent revising and devising new ideas so that the universal energy system continues to expand.

When the energies from the planet Earth have begun the releasing process there will be a time of complete darkness. This will last only a matter of days, but cannot be allowed to be any other way. There will be much confusion when this occurs. The energies will continue to be released, but will be abated through the energy from other planets. We cannot give you specific timings for this process. The energies will release when all parts of the plan are centred. The energies are needed throughout the underworld of your planet. It is a process of rejuvenation.

Throughout the inner workings of the planet Earth there has become much clogging and dismantling of the finer network of energy control. This will be altered when the frequency becomes higher than the highest energy present. We can only now give you the briefest of understanding, as you do not have the capacity to allow your minds to become free of all of the barriers you have erected. It is the finer tuning of energies that will enable your planet to take her rightful position within the universal system. We cannot now alter her course, it has been ordained.

Qu: Which planets will be involved in the re-tuning of our planet Earth?
It will be from the planets of Mars and Uranus that much of the energy will be received. The energies from these two planets will be in a conjunction during these times of energising.

Qu: How will we be affected when the asteroid reaches Jupiter in July of this year?
After July of this year the energy of Jupiter will be affected. We cannot give you exact locations of this collision, but will be able to give you much of the information preceding this event by some weeks. If the collision occurs within the south side of Jupiter, then there will be much energy released within the vicinity of the planet Earth. We cannot give exact amounts, but this energy will only assist the rebirthing of the planet Earth. She will not become affected in a physical manner, but will be given a boost of energy which could propel the actions of the ascension process into a further crescendo. There are many effects which may be felt, but will not be known until the area of collision is completely datarised.

Energy that has been received from Jupiter will become of a different calibre. It will not be of the nature of which you are used. The energy from Jupiter will be changed wherever the asteroid falls. If you begin now to approach the idea of collision with the viewpoint of energy, you will understand a lot more of the outcome. During a collision there are many changes, that of energy being the most powerful.

It would be good for you to remember what it is like if someone bangs you on the head. You do not just feel the physical touch; you are immobilised for many minutes through the energy collisions that occur within the whole of your head. As your head becomes the object of collision, so Jupiter will become the object of the blows of the asteroid. During a bang on the head, you may see stars as are depicted within your comic strips. These stars are the feelings and visual sights that you see as energy becomes part of the reaction from the collision. There will be many stars and visual reactions for the planet Jupiter. This displacement of energy from around the planet will be generated out into the universal system.

For some the energy from the planets has a diverse effect within their makeup. There are some that can carry the energies of the planets and use this to the utmost good. We cannot say that all of you will be affected with the same vibrations. It will be the same energy that descends upon your planet Earth. But the energies will be used differently by the energies that are already present around your own auric fields. If you receive direct energy transference from the planet Jupiter, then you will be able to complete your tasks and missions very much faster. There will be much stress to those who have not begun their spiritual development. The energy from Jupiter has been a great innovator for many of you. It will be as if there has been a great calamity within their systems when the second stage is activated before the first

After the explosion on the planet Jupiter there will be many different reactions within the heavens. Some of these happenings will cause other strange phenomena to be present upon the planet Earth. When we speak of phenomena we are talking about the presence of other energies within the field of the earth plane. You cannot at the moment begin to comprehend what these energies are and what will indeed come about. If we were to approach all of these different complex energy phenomena, it would indeed take us a very long time, but we will insist upon the information being available for you as soon as this is needed.

The energies that will be upon you from the onset of the energy releases are the ones that you will be concerned about. During this period there will be delay with information for we too will be affected when the ravaging energies are being released.

After this period the contact that we have with you will be completely direct – by this we mean that the interference levels will be extinct. You will be able to converse with us as if we were with you in a physical existence. We will indeed be there, but not in a form that will be compatible with your own physicality. We do not mean to infer that we cannot be with you, but that the gaps will still be present between our form and yours.

We have spoken before of the time to come when for some there will be much confusion, and indeed stress, connected with the energy that will be needed to maintain the body in a healthy condition. We cannot stress enough the need to begin to control your thought patterns, and indeed everything that you do within the planes of your Earth planet. If you do not heed our warnings, your bodies will still require to be within the Third dimensional energy fields which will by this time be over. If you cannot maintain the energies within your own bodies, then you will begin to experience a great deal of stress and bodily toxicity.

During this time of cleansing much will be experienced. If you cannot now deal with the changes and mishaps within your field of experience, then of course you will never maintain your balance when the Earth upheavals are upon you. Everything within the energy field of the planet Earth will begin to change. Everything within your own field of experience will alter. If you have begun to experience the changes, then you will also begin to alter your code of expectancy. Those that have begun to realise that there will be changes will indeed expect them.

From now onwards towards the time of ascension of the planet Earth, nothing will be as you have expected it to be. We speak now of your expectancy within the code of practice that has been experienced within your earth field before. Now is the time for all of your expectancies to be counteracted by the knowledge that anything is possible and that everything will be ok. This ok has many different explanations. It is when there is nothing that can harm you. If you have stood within the earth planes when we were talking to you, then you know already that it has not been as has been explained to you that you were alone in this part of the galaxy.

Energy will be given to you in order for you to be able to maintain the forces required to abdicate now from these earthly ties. You are not of these dimensions, there is much energy available for you to realise these facts. We speak of facts, ones that have not been realised within the restrictions of your earthly planes.

Much of the information needed will be given. There are many different ways that we have of communicating with you. When you are free and open we will allow the energy of our planes to be with you. We cannot always maintain this contact for long periods of time because of the mind frequencies that interfere with our linkage with you. It is because of your attachment to these earthly planes that our connections with you are made impossible in some cases and very scanty in others.

Part of the divine plan has been the comradeship of many different species of being. We are all of the same essence, but we come in different ways and forms. Some are very distinctive in their code of practice. They will be upon your planes when the energies release. You will experience their energy when the energy of the planet Earth reaches the extreme proportions of which we have spoken. The energies of these beings will be able to balance out some of the areas which have negativity entrenched deep within the very core of the Earth. These energy beings are extremely powerful and will be assisting the continuum of universal energy through allowing these energies to pass over the earth plane.

We speak of many different species of beings that have been called upon to be part of these divine occurrences. We do not need to give you their identities. There have been many different types of energy that have evolved within the quarters of the Universe. These types will be evolving throughout the next period of time in order to be of service. Very often there will be swarms of different energy organisms that will descend upon the planet Earth in order to balance and counterbalance any of the extreme disturbances. We cannot now alter any of this plan.

It will be sufficient for your armies to be amongst us to realise that there will be peace. The plan does not involve any of the fighting that has begun in different pockets around your planet, but because of the energy transference we are seeing that negativity is being released through this form of communication. It is only a form of communication. We are aware of its negative form, but will say that it is better to have this form of communication than none at all. If we were to abandon our courage now, we would not see the dawning of your new day and could not then approach any of our other planets with this plan for evolvement and salvation.

Some of the disturbances around your planet Earth have begun because of the negativity that has been building for centuries. It is only now that they have the courage to begin to ask for what they really deserve. The energies will not be able to secure the state of peace for you until all of the negativity has been released. We cannot give you the ultimate union with God your Maker and your fellow man until there has been the completion of the cleansing process. If you are expecting to begin the next day with complete and utter union, then we have not educated you enough yet!

When the Sun begins to give out her solar rays, the energy will be first of molecular structure, and then as time goes by the energy releases around the molecule and changes into a helium energy force field. If we could instruct all of your scientists and physicists in the ways of the Universe, then there would be no panic and no fear, for they would have begun to plan for the time ahead. But alas, the contact that has been made with a few scientists has not been sufficient for them to have any real effect within these fields.

When this helium energy is received within the stratosphere of the planet Earth it has a molecular structure which does not compare with any other energy within your energy field. We have therefore needed to cooperate with this energy so that the energy does not damage the forcefield of the atmosphere. In doing so, we have given you the ozone layer, now that this layer has been damaged, the energy from the helium molecules are changing everything within its force field. Each day there have been changes within your Earth field. Each day the energy that you are receiving will be different.

We cannot attempt to give you the energy equations, but will attempt to open the areas of your minds that have decided that the information you have been given is correct. Any of the information that has been given to these areas of your minds has been severely colonised. We promise that our objectives for your existence within this area of the Universe are totally and absolutely of the purest kind.

The energy that has been given to you will allow the minds of men to become of the universal kind. We are here attempting to allow the minds of men to become at one with the energies of the Universe. If we do not attempt this then what will come about will be of mankind's own making. He will not survive within the universal energy continuum.

The universal energy continuum operates solely upon the golden rays of the Master energies. In this way everything becomes 'one'. If we were to speak to you now of this continuum it would be 'mind-blowing'. During the period of changes there will be many that do not survive, but also there will be those that do. It will be much to do with the energies of these peoples, as to whether they are in fact able to exist within this new energy field.

Very soon after the changes there will be a time of light. During this time many will become totally and absolutely merged with the light. It will be as if the light of Jesus Christ is upon your planet and indeed He will be there. During this time it will be very much a case of those who grow towards the light will become in tune with the Masters and any of the other beings who will gather around the planet Earth. This light has masterful qualities. It will lead you back to your spiritual mantles.

Qu: What is meant by the title of this section – The Movement of the Sun in front of the Moon and Stars?
What we are giving you is the fact that the Sun will be prominent in the heavens. At the moment, the Sun may be indeed the brightest light that you have within the vicinity of the planet Earth, but you will also be able to see many other lights from the stars and planets that are within the heavens, and indeed the Moon. There will be a time when the Sun does in fact move towards the planet Earth and will indeed cover the Moon and the stars. This does not mean that the

energy of the Sun will consume the planet Earth, but that the energy
of the Sun will become very much more prominent.

*Qu: Earlier on in this manuscript you have said that the Sun will split in
two. Is this why the energy of the Sun will become more prominent?*
Yes, the energy of the Sun will be split into two different fractions.
This will only occur because of the heavens changing. The changes
that will occur in the heavens will cause many of the stars and planets
to change their orbits. During this period there will be a time when,
because of the deflection of the energies of the Sun, you will experience two different sources of this energy. There will be one source
that comes directly from the Sun herself and another source that is
given to you through deflection.

*Qu: How does this deflection process work, does it involve any of the planets
that we see now?*
Yes, it will involve the planets of Scorpio, also the planets of Sagit-
tarius and Uranus. This will begin when the energy of the planet
Earth has reached her peak. During the great upheavals on your
planet Earth, there will also be great upheavals within the heavens.
Many of the planets that you see now will not be seen. There will be a
time when none of the planets are seen. The deflection process
involves many of the areas of the solar system that are not known to
you.

Qu: Are there any more actual facts that we need to know on this event?
The facts are startling for your minds, but as time goes by, you will
be able to see that everything is changeable. For many years you have
existed within the very narrow dimensions of the planet Earth. It is as
if you have been sealed inside an incubator, only aware of what was
going on inside. You could have asked before, 'How does this incubator function; what are the outside influences that control my very
existence?' If we had left you inside the incubator, there would have
been a time when the energy from the incubator would have blown
the insides outside.

Do not distress yourselves with thoughts of regret. Those things and
ideas from your past can all be put behind you now. If you are held

into the memories of your pasts then none of you will reach forward towards the new horizons.

Plato talked, in his lifetime, of the cave. If you were still in that cave you would all be dead. During the last decade there has been movement outside the cave, and some of the people who have cut themselves from their shackles are returning over and over again to rescue others who had not the knowledge of how to cut themselves free. There will be many who cut themselves free during this present year. Others who have stayed longer in the cave will become aware as they realise that many are leaving. The impulses of change are upon you.

Plato did not think it possible to go back and instruct others as to the wonders outside the cave. In Plato's time on your planet Earth this was not possible. It would be very much more possible in this day because of the timing and the energy that is present upon your planet Earth. We cannot understand now why so many of you have stayed within the confines of the cave walls, but we have compassion for you and will be here to cheer as you do now decide to release yourselves. There is always a safety within the confines of what you know and understand, but there is also a denigration of spiritual awareness.

Others who have not stepped outside the cave will begin to wonder why they have been left. When they begin to wonder, of course this will also serve as a catalyst. During the time inside the cave when they were with all of their friends, they did not have to use the thought of wonderment.

Understanding does not always carry the true grit. It is sometimes much easier to give up understanding and allow the power of your creative minds to give you truth. When all has been revealed, you will feel like you never ever had any understanding. Do not put any acclaim to this word 'understanding'; it will not serve you well over the next few years. When you have opened up the full capacity of your creative minds then you will be able to say 'I know'. It will be when you have joined with the universal energy continuum that you will also be able to acclaim 'I understand'. It will not be easy for you to begin to understand until you have had an experience of what is actually being spoken of.

As usual we cannot serve your intellects, but can only hope that through reading our words, you will begin to awaken to the great joys and peace that await you in this, your New World.